Routledge Revivals

The Giants of Asia

First published in 1967, *The Giants of Asia* discusses the growth of Asian nationalism and Asian power. It surveys the major Asian countries and the three major forms that Asian nationalism has taken: constitutional democracy in India and initially in Pakistan, the pre-war militarism of Japan, and nationalist communism in China. The author discusses the problems of unity and government after the withdrawal of European power. He has been extraordinarily successful in conveying unfamiliar ideas concretely and simply—in surveying this vast unfamiliar field with simple clarity. This book will be of interest to students and researchers of politics, history, and Asian studies.

The Giants of Asia

India, Pakistan, China, Japan

Stephen Hugh-Jones

Routledge
Taylor & Francis Group

First published in 1967
by George Allen and Unwin Ltd

This edition first published in 2024 by Routledge
4 Park Square, Milton Park, Abingdon, Oxon, OX14 4RN

and by Routledge
605 Third Avenue, New York, NY 10017

Routledge is an imprint of the Taylor & Francis Group, an informa business

Publisher's Note
The publisher has gone to great lengths to ensure the quality of this reprint but points out that some imperfections in the original copies may be apparent.

Disclaimer
The publisher has made every effort to trace copyright holders and welcomes correspondence from those they have been unable to contact.

A Library of Congress record exists under LCCN: 68088693

ISBN: 978-1-032-88848-4 (hbk)
ISBN: 978-1-003-53996-4 (ebk)
ISBN: 978-1-032-88850-7 (pbk)

Book DOI 10.4324/9781003539964

THE GIANTS OF ASIA

India, Pakistan, China, Japan

BY

STEPHEN HUGH-JONES

B.A.

London
GEORGE ALLEN AND UNWIN LTD
RUSKIN HOUSE MUSEUM STREET

THE AUTHOR studied at Oxford, was formerly Foreign Editor of the *Indian Express*, Bombay and now works in the foreign department of *The Economist*, specializing in Asian affairs.

ACKNOWLEDGEMENTS
The author and publishers gratefully acknowledge the help of the following in the provision of pictures: Central News Service, Taipeh, Fig. 15; *Dorchester Times,* Dorchester-on-Thames, Fig. 1; Hsinhua News Agency, Figs. 10, 13, 14, 21; Indian High Commission, London, Figs. 2, 3, 16, 18, 19, 20; Japanese Embassy, London, Fig. 22; Pakistani High Commission, London, Figs. 11, 17; Radio Times Hulton Picture Library, Figs. 5, 6, 7, 8, 9, 12; H.M. Secretary of State for the Commonwealth, Fig. 4.

FIRST PUBLISHED IN 1967

PRINTED IN GREAT BRITAIN
in 11 point Times Roman type
BY JARROLD & SONS LTD, NORWICH

CONTENTS

A note to teachers

1. Outlook. The aim of this book is to prepare pupils for the world in which they are growing up. Its standpoint therefore is specifically that of the present day; and its theme, in consequence, the replacement of European power in Asia by that of Asian nationalism. This is 'the history of the victors'; later perspectives will no doubt outdate it, and it demands a selection of facts that must seem unfair to the losers. The author has run both risks in the belief that it is more valuable for young Westerners to understand how Asians see Asia's recent past today than to be offered a guess how history will see it tomorrow or to be told, yet again, how the West saw it yesterday.

2. Concepts. Many concepts here are either unfamiliar in British politics (e.g. communism, militarism, mass organization, force) or so familiar (such as democracy or freedom) that Britons seldom realize their full meaning or how unnatural, outside the Western world, they are. These will need more explanation – starting from the principle that Asia is *different* – than the author has had space for.

3. Names. All Asian names here should be pronounced as they are spelt, the vowels having their 'international' values (as in Italian) rather than their English ones; Chou En-lai, for instance, is, roughly, *Joe En-lye,* not *Chow En-lay*. In Chinese personal names, the surname comes first; in Indian and Pakistani names, last. This book follows the normal Western (but not Japanese) custom of putting Japanese surnames also last.

1. EUROPE AND ASIA

Asia is important

There are 52 million people in Great Britain, 11 million in Australia, only 4 million in Ireland. But in Japan there are 100 million, in India 500 million, in China 750 million.

Two thousand years ago most of the people in Britain were savages. But in China and India there were rich kingdoms, well-built towns, writers and sculptors whose work is admired today.

We Europeans often think of our countries as if they were the centre of the world, the place where all the important inventions were made, where science, art and music were developed, where all the history that really mattered happened.

We are utterly wrong. The great countries of Asia were important long before ours were. They may well one day again be far more important than ours.

That is the first thing to learn about them.

But Asia has learned from the West

Yet in one way we are right. The world today is a world that has been shaped by Western (European or American) ideas and Western science. The Japanese today make superb cameras; but the camera was invented in Europe. India's parliament is an imitation of Britain's. China, the biggest country in the world, is ruled by communists; communism is based on the ideas of Karl Marx – a German who lived in London.

Why is this? It is because for several centuries, roughly from 1500 to 1900, the people of the Western world were more imaginative, more adventurous, richer, and eventually more powerful, than any others.

1. *Southern and Eastern Asia*

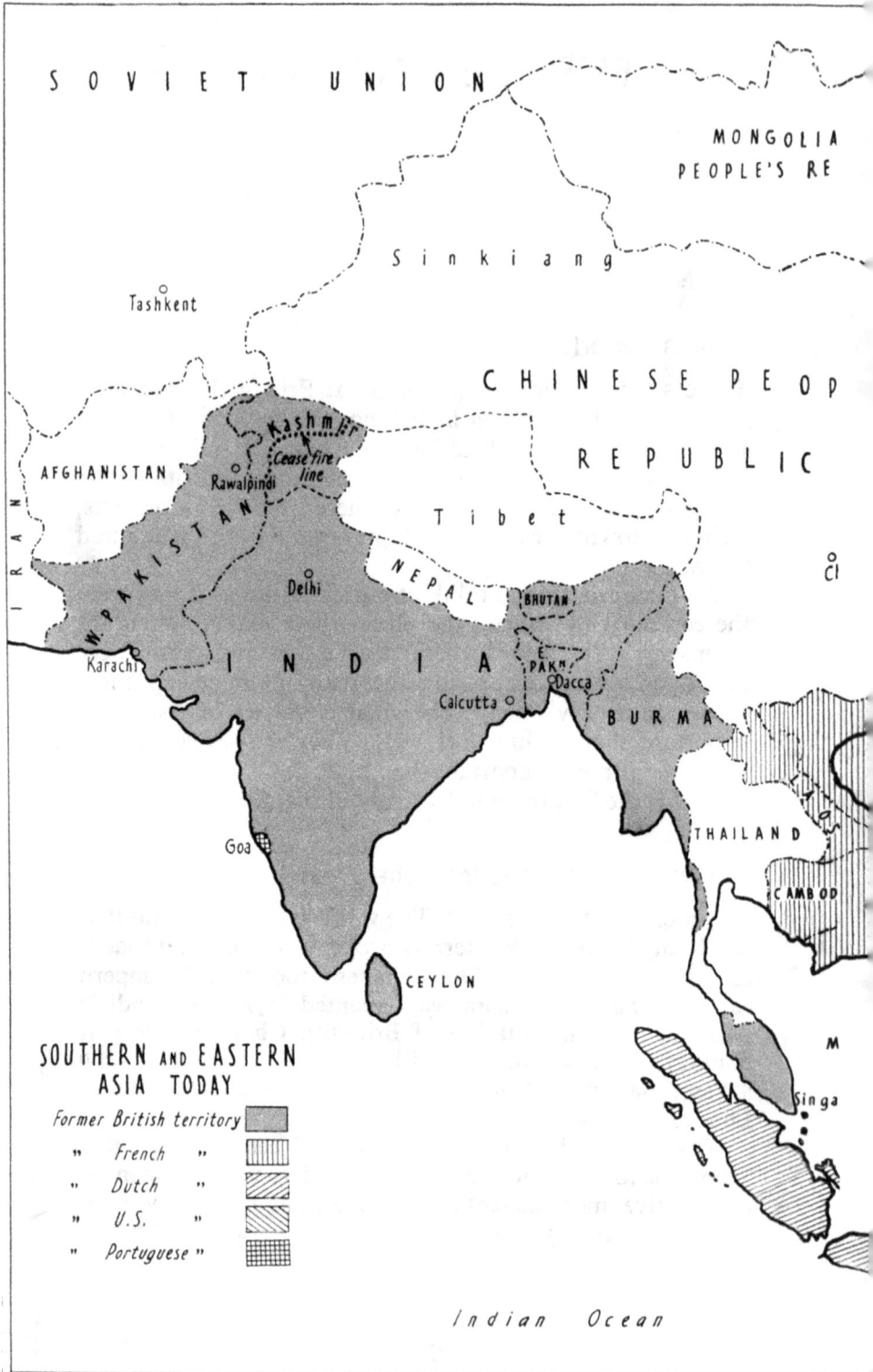

SOVIET UNION

MONGOLIA
PEOPLE'S RE

Sinkiang

Tashkent

CHINESE PEOp

REPUBLIC

AFGHANISTAN

Kashmir

Cease fire
line

Rawalpindi

W PAKISTAN

Tibet

NEPAL

BHUTAN

Delhi

I N D I A

E
PAKN
Dacca

Calcutta

BURMA

Karachi

Goa

THAILAND

CAMBOD

CEYLON

M

SOUTHERN AND EASTERN
ASIA TODAY

Former British territory
" French "
" Dutch "
" U.S. "
" Portuguese "

Sin ga

Indian Ocean

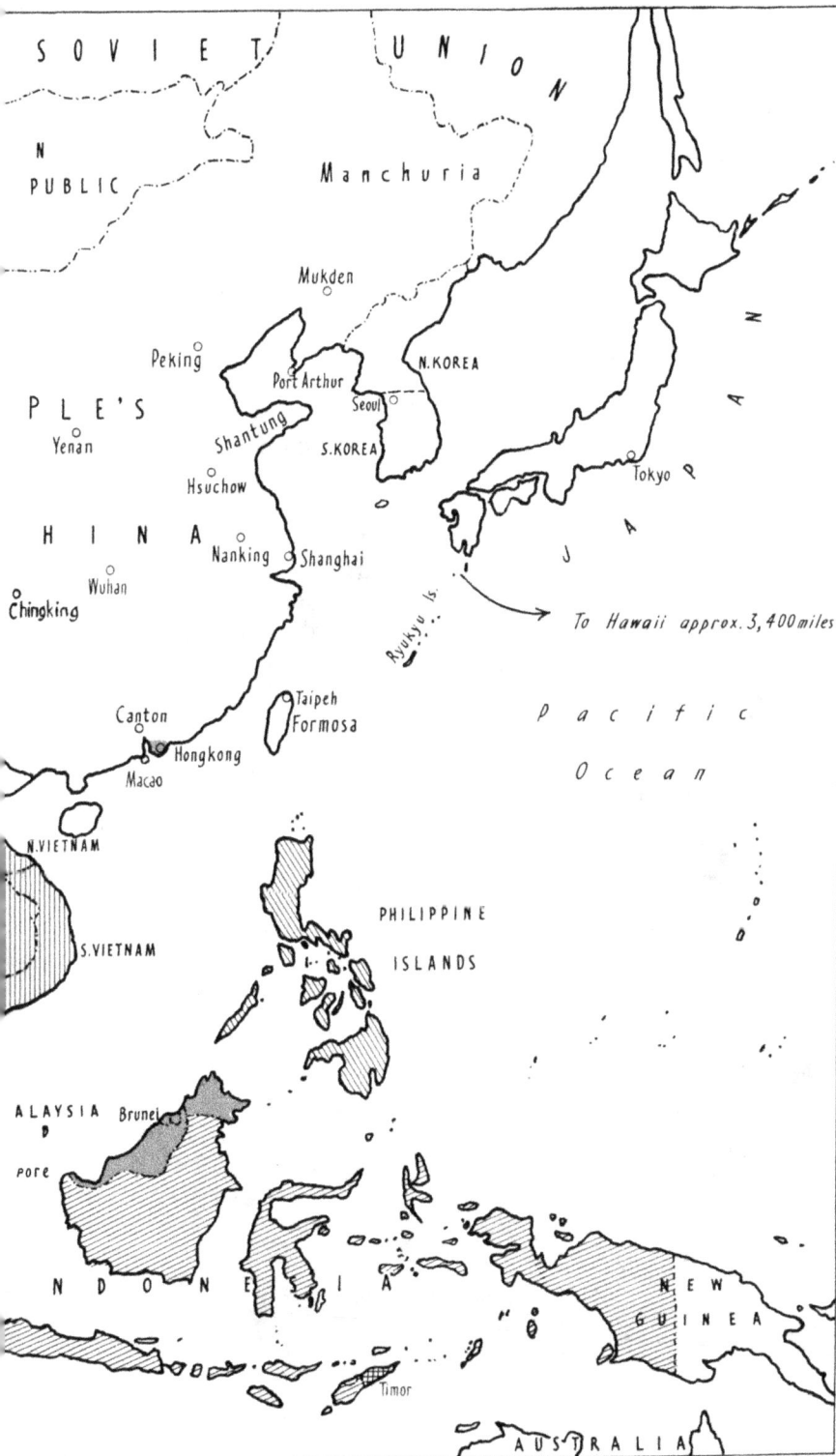

How the Europeans won their empires

Ships carrying merchants, missionaries or soldiers set out from Portugal, Spain, Holland, France and Britain to the most distant parts of the world. Sometimes the Europeans were drowned or killed. But always more came after them.

Some of the countries they discovered were richer and more powerful than their own – at first. In the eighteenth century, Englishmen in India admired the wealth of the princes, and the beautiful cottons and silks woven there. But back in Britain, inventors were making machines to weave cloth, and steam-engines to drive them. Soon Lancashire mills were weaving by machine, while Indians were still weaving by hand. Lancashire became rich. India became poor.

In China, one emperor thought British ships arriving there had come to bring a humble message from some barbarian chief. Why not? The Chinese had invented many things before Europeans had ever heard of them. Gunpowder, for instance. But it was the Europeans who learned to use explosives in rifles and machine-guns. When Chinese fought Europeans, it was the Europeans who won.

1. *This was how the Europeans won their empires; and this was the idea of Asia they came to have in their minds. A history book of 1803 shows a British soldier killing Tippoo Saib, an Indian prince – described as a 'tyrant' – a few years before*

Asians were humiliated

The Europeans were cunning, strong and ruthless. If they could not get what they wanted by talking, or with money, they eventually tried to take it by force. Usually they succeeded. So Europe acquired the empires of which Europeans were so proud.

But for Asians the great days of the British or Dutch empires were days of shame and humiliation. For them this was 'the age of European imperialism', one that they have not forgotten and often not forgiven.

Europeans today might well ask whether their ancestors were worse than anyone else. Throughout history strong nations have crushed weak ones. Within the last thirty years Japanese, Chinese and Indians have behaved as savagely as the European empire-builders ever did.

Asians remember their humiliation

The obvious lesson is that any nation or race can behave well, or badly. But that is not the lesson most Asians draw from their history – and to understand Asia one must understand what Asians think, and why they think it.

To Europeans, the story of their empires, now that it is almost ended, is something of a sideline. But to Asians it is a central fact of their history.

What they remember is that their countries were attacked and conquered by foreigners. Their languages and religions and ways of life were despised. They were looked down on simply for not being white-skinned. Their industries were controlled by foreigners, and Asia stayed poor while Europe grew rich.

This is certainly not the whole truth – the Europeans did good things as well – but it is an important part of the truth. And it is the part that Asians tend to remember.

India, China and Japan

Asia's three great countries – India, China and Japan – all had experience of the European adventurers. But each had a different experience, and reacted differently.

India (meaning the whole area which in 1947 was divided

into two countries, India and Pakistan) was conquered by the
British, and ruled by them for nearly 200 years.

China in the nineteenth century just, but only just, escaped
being divided up by several greedy European countries.

Japan refused to let the first tiny settlements of Europeans
grow larger, as happened in other Asian countries. So Japan
was able to remain free. Later it was the first Asian country to
stand up as an equal to the Europeans and Americans.

Each of these countries in turn – first Japan, then India, then
China – and each in its different way played the chief part,
between 1941 and 1955, in ending the European age in Asia.

Let us look at each in turn. To start with, India.

2. *A large Hindu temple in south India. The tower is covered with
painted statues of Hindu gods*

2. THE RELIGIONS OF INDIA

The importance of religion

Religion is very important in India. For centuries there have been two religious groups there, Hindus and Muslims. When 'British' India became free in 1947 it was split into two countries: India, whose people are mainly Hindus, and Pakistan, which was specially created as a home for Muslims.

Hinduism

Hinduism is the ancient religion of India. Hindus worship many different gods, and make idols of them. They believe that a person is reborn many times, and that what he does in one life will decide what state he is born into in the next. He may be born to be a priest or to be a roadsweeper, and if he is 'unlucky' he must just accept it; it is his own fault.

This idea is reflected in the Hindu caste system. There are many castes – of priests or fishermen or blacksmiths, for instance – and each one has its proper place in society. Members of a caste do not necessarily all do the same kind of work. But they stick together, help each other, usually marry each other, and nowadays often vote for each other regardless of political party.

The minor religions

Today there are several small religious groups in India: Parsees, Buddhists, Christians and Jews. There are also the Sikhs, whose religion is a kind of purified Hinduism. Though they are only a few million, they are important because most of them live on the border between India and Pakistan.

The Muslims

The other important group is the Muslims. Their religion, called Islam, is much more like Christianity. They believe in one God. Their holy book is the Koran, which, they believe, contains the very words that God revealed to his Prophet Mohammed, an Arab who lived about 1,300 years ago. They have no idols or statues of saints. Like Christians – but unlike Hindus – they think their religion is better than any other, and try to convert people to it.

Differences between Hindus and Muslims

This religion reached India about 1,200 years ago, but first became important about A.D. 1100. It was brought in by Muslim invaders from the west, and many Hindus were forcibly, or willingly, converted to it. The Hindu and Muslim communities usually, though not always, lived peacefully side by side. But they never became one community.

3. *The great Muslim mosque in Delhi built more than 300 years ago by the Muslim emperors who then ruled India*

They have many different customs. For instance, Muslims sacrifice cows on certain holy days, and cheerfully eat beef. Hindus regard the cow as something to be treated with great respect, and very few Hindus will touch beef. Both Hindus and Muslims may use the same spoken language, Hindustani. But they write it in different scripts. Even today, when many of the old customs are being forgotten, it is almost unknown for a Hindu and a Muslim to marry.

Why British India was split

This religious difference is the clue to much of what has happened in modern India. The struggle for India's freedom was a struggle between Britain and India. But hidden beneath it there was another struggle, between Indians: between Indian Hindus and Indian Muslims. And the more obvious it became that the struggle against the British would be won, the more this other struggle came into the open. That is why India had to be split into two separate countries.

The British are often blamed for having tried to 'divide and rule' by encouraging disagreements between their Hindu and Muslim subjects. That is partly true. But it is also true that they could not have encouraged this Hindu-Muslim rivalry if it had not already existed.

3. THE BRITISH IN INDIA

How the British won their empire

When the first British merchants arrived in India about 300 years ago, the country, though mainly Hindu, was governed by Muslim emperors from Delhi in north India. But by 1750 this empire was breaking up. The British, who had come to trade, began to acquire power and territory. By allying themselves with one Indian prince against another, they gradually extended their control. By 1856 they controlled almost the whole of India. Indians have never forgotten that it was their own disunity that gave Britain its chance.

How they behaved in it

The early British merchants were in India for money. But even among them there were some who had a real respect for Indian culture and religion, and Indian ways of life. They treated Indians as equals.

But from about 1840 onwards, this attitude began to change. The British began to ask themselves, now that they governed such huge areas of a foreign land, *why* they were doing so. This was a time of tremendous self-confidence in Britain. Industry and science were advancing rapidly. British society, which had been as corrupt as any other, began to be reformed. Under the influence of Christians, it began to be seriously believed that those who were rich and powerful had a duty to help those who were not.

The British in India naturally applied these new standards there. They saw around them the misgovernment and corruption of the old Indian rulers. They were certain the British way of life was better. They decided it was their duty to bring its benefits to India, to teach Indians British standards of government, justice, education, and science.

That, they said, was why they were governing India.

The British grow proud

That was the theory. But what actually happened was often much less high-minded. And there were other reasons for governing India that were purely selfish: for instance, that it made a splendid new market for British goods. But even at its best the theory assumed that British ways were better than Indian ones, and that it was right to force them on India, whether the Indians wanted them or not.

In short, it assumed that Englishmen were better than Indians.

The Indians grow resentful

Indians naturally disliked being treated as inferiors. And the British did two things that weakened their own position. One was to help Hindus learn about India's past. British and other European scholars studied India's ancient languages and culture. Many Hindus had forgotten these things, or rejected them in favour of the new ideas from the West. Now, as they learned more about their own country, they learned to be proud of it.

Still more important, Indians learned about British liberalism and parliamentary democracy. These were new ideas in India, and many Indians were glad that the British had brought them. But they were soon disappointed. They found that the British did not practise what they preached, except at home. They seemed to be saying that democracy was all right for Englishmen in England, but not for Indians in India.

At least, not yet. Even in those days, some British officials looked forward to the day when India would be 'fit' for self-government. But they saw that day a long way off. Indians, after a time, reckoned it should be just round the corner.

So a struggle developed between the British officials and the educated Indian politicians; not about *whether* the British would eventually quit India, but *when*.

4. THE INDIAN FREEDOM MOVEMENT

Growth of the freedom movement

The national movement which eventually forced the British to quit India was the Indian National Congress (generally known simply as Congress). It became a mass political party, with revolutionary aims: to overthrow British power in India.

Yet when it was first formed, in 1885, it was a small 'respectable' middle-class group which proclaimed its loyalty to British rule. The man who inspired it was an Englishman living in India.

How and why did it change?

Moderates and Extremists

The first change arose from a split within Congress between a 'moderate' and an 'extremist' group, which began in the 1890s.

The 'moderates' greatly valued British rule in India. What they wanted was that Indians should take more part in it, so that, after an 'apprenticeship', they would be fit to govern themselves. The 'moderates' valued British liberal ideas. They hoped to win their way by persuasion, by showing that Indians could be as loyal citizens, and as effective in public life, as Englishmen.

The 'extremists' opposed British rule. They rejected the idea of 'apprenticeship' to the British. They looked back to the great days of Indian history, and appealed to religious patriotism – that is to *Hindu* religious feeling. Above all, they rejected the notion of persuading the British into giving way by loyal co-operation and argument. If you want freedom, they said, take it. Boycott British goods and buy Indian ones. Refuse to pay taxes. Disobey laws.

In 1907 the 'extremists' and 'moderates' finally split. The 'extremists', who were in a minority, left Congress. In 1908 their leader, B. G. Tilak (1856–1920) was sentenced to six years' imprisonment for sedition. The 'moderates' seemed to be in command.

But in 1914 Tilak was released, and in 1915 the great 'moderate' leader G. K. Gokhale (1866–1915) died. The 'extremists' rejoined Congress and in 1916 captured control.

Gandhi and Congress

But Congress was still a middle-class group. The man who turned it into a mass political movement was M. K. Gandhi (1869–1948), sometimes known as *Mahatma* ('great soul') Gandhi. Indians call him 'the father of the nation' and some regard him almost as a saint.

Muslims begin to fear Hindus

To understand his life, we must see what had happened to the relationship between Muslims and Hindus. It was the split between them that caused India to be partitioned in 1947. And Gandhi, though he tried to prevent this split, helped to cause it.

The Muslims had begun by 1900 to be alarmed at the growth of Congress, which was dominated by Hindus. They feared that democratic government would mean Hindu government, since Hindus outnumbered Muslims three to one. In 1906 they formed a Muslim League. They asked that if any democratic system was introduced, there should be separate electorates for Hindus and Muslims (that is, that there should be 'members of parliament' elected only by Muslim voters and others elected only by Hindus).

When the first steps towards democracy were taken in 1909 (the 'Morley-Minto reforms'), this was granted. The reasons were mixed. The British genuinely felt there was some justification for the fears of the Muslims. But they also saw that it would suit the government very nicely to keep its Indian subjects divided.

But in 1916, everything seemed to change. The First World

War had broken out in 1914. At first there was great enthusiasm in India for the British cause. But then Britain went to war with Turkey, a Muslim country. Muslims recognized the Sultan of Turkey as the Caliph ('leader') of Islam.

Congress and the Muslim League agreed in 1916 to co-operate together. The agreement was largely brought about by Mohammed Ali Jinnah (1876–1948), a Muslim lawyer who for some time had been a member of Congress and was now an independent. No one foresaw that he would later lead the fight against Congress to create a separate homeland for Muslims, Pakistan.

Gandhi returns to India

Gandhi's career in India began in 1915, when he came back after many years in South Africa. He had gone there, after studying in England, in 1893. He found that he, and all other Indians, were ill-treated because they were not white. He became the champion of the Indians against the white South Africans.

But he did not believe in violent opposition. He believed in persuasion, and, if that did not work, in peaceful non-co-operation, 'civil disobedience' as he called it; for instance, refusing to obey unjust laws. The right method, he said, was not force but *satyagraha* – 'truth-force'.

When he returned to India, he first took an interest in helping the poorest peasants and workers. He was enthusiastically loyal to the British. But in time he decided that they did not deserve loyalty. It was the British administrators who tried to stop him doing good and who demanded taxes from people who could not afford to pay them.

The Amritsar massacre

In 1917, the British government in London declared that their aim was, eventually, to create a form of government in India controlled by the people, just as in Britain. But at the same time the (British) government of India made new laws giving itself greater power to stop 'subversive' activity. Gandhi organized what Indians call *hartal* – a complete stoppage of all work and business – against these laws.

There were demonstrations and riots against the government. In 1919, at Amritsar, in north India, when a forbidden meeting was being held, British troops broke it up by shooting. Nearly 400 people were killed, and hundreds more wounded. This terrible action turned Indians more strongly than ever against the British. But Gandhi, preaching non-violence, helped to prevent a rebellion breaking out.

The first non-co-operation movement

The British now made new laws (the 'Montagu-Chelmsford reforms') that would give more power to elected governments in India's eleven provinces. But Congress, led by Gandhi, refused to co-operate or to take part in the elections.

At the same time the government was threatened by a Muslim movement called the *Khilafat* ('Caliphate') movement. Indian Muslims had been angered at the treaty after the First World War, that broke up the empire of the Sultan of Turkey, the Caliph. Led by two brothers (the Ali brothers) they threatened to rebel. But instead Gandhi persuaded them to join his Congress non-co-operation movement.

For a time Hindus and Muslims were united in a campaign of non-violence against the British. But the non-co-operation did not always stay non-violent (this indeed happened to every supposedly non-violent movement that Congress ever organized). In 1922, after twenty-two people had been burned to death in a police station by a mob, Gandhi suddenly called the campaign off. His Congress and Muslim allies were dismayed. He might almost have lost his leadership. But the British saved him by arresting him and sentencing him to six years in prison (of which he actually served two).

The end of the campaign left Hindus and Muslims free to quarrel with each other. Already in 1921 the Hindus had been appalled by a Muslim uprising in south India (the Moplah Rebellion) which turned into violence – against Hindus. In 1924 the Turkish government itself abolished the Caliphate, and the *Khilafat* movement collapsed.

Results of the movement

So by the end of 1924 three important things had happened.

  1. The Indian nationalists had successfully launched their

first mass movement of non-co-operation against the British.

2. But they had been – or felt they had been – utterly defeated when Gandhi called it off.

3. Congress and the Muslims had parted company, for good.

5. GANDHI: POLITICIAN, REFORMER, SAINT

Gandhi the politician

Though the first non-co-operation movement did not succeed, it set the pattern of Indian politics for the next twenty-five years. Its results reflect both Gandhi's skill and his weakness as a politician.

He knew exactly how to arouse the common people. He did simple, dramatic things which they understood. He himself lived in poverty. He wore ordinary Indian clothes, not European ones as most of the middle-class politicians did. He used to spin the cotton for his own clothes, and chose the spinning-wheel (something that most poor Indians would have known from childhood) as the symbol of Indian freedom from British industries, the proof that Indians, doing things in an Indian way, could stand on their own feet.

He was greatly helped by being deeply religious and very deeply Hindu. Yet this also meant that while he appealed to Hindu peasants, Muslims were put off. And it was exactly because he converted Congress into a mass party, depending on the (mainly Hindu) masses, that the Muslims came to distrust it.

Gandhi's non-co-operation was a brilliant method of involving large numbers of people actively in the political struggle for freedom; and yet of avoiding deliberate violence that might lead to revolution (which Gandhi did not want and which would have frightened off many middle-class supporters). But this was also a weakness. Gandhi was ready to challenge the government, but not to carry the fight through to the end.

He believed (wrongly) that the British would give way before the power of his 'truth-force'. They did – up to a point; after that point they began using violence.

So the government became frightened by Gandhi's challenge and delayed reforms. But it was never actually forced into giving way. It is possible, though far from certain, that India would have become free sooner (and as one country, not two) if Gandhi had never existed, and if the fight had been carried out either by revolution alone or by argument alone, not by methods in between.

Gandhi the social reformer

Gandhi was not only a politician. He was a social reformer. He saw many things wrong with the Hindu way of life. He insisted that the 'untouchables' – people below the bottom of the Hindu caste system – must be treated as equals. They must be allowed to enter the same temples and use the same wells as high-caste Hindus.

4. *Official India. The Viceroy and his staff meet an Indian prince and his staff, at the prince's palace, some time in the 1920s*

Gandhi believed that everything could be changed if only people would change the way they behaved. They should follow truth and love and non-violence, and give up their interest in money, food and comfort. Gandhi could do this himself, but he did not always realize that for most people it was too difficult. But they respected him greatly for what he said, and for actually practising what he preached.

Although he was a Hindu, Gandhi had no prejudice whatever against people of any other religion. When there was violence between Hindus and Muslims, he often risked his reputation, and sometimes his life, to save Muslims from harm. In the end he was murdered, in 1948, for that very reason by a fanatical Hindu.

5. *Unofficial India. Gandhi demonstrates spinning at a public meeting in 1925*

Gandhi's personality was very powerful. He inspired devotion in his political colleagues even when they disagreed with him. His enemies respected him as they respected no other Congress leader. This is what the English judge who condemned Gandhi to six years in prison said to him before doing so:

'You are in a different category from any person I have tried or am likely to try. In the eyes of millions of your countrymen you are a great patriot and a great leader. Even those who differ from you in politics look upon you as a man of high ideals and of noble and even saintly life.'

6. CONGRESS AGAINST BRITAIN

Congress and elections

After the collapse of the non-co-operation movement in 1922, what was Congress to do next? Some leaders, notably Motilal Nehru, a north Indian lawyer, argued that it should take advantage of the 'Montagu-Chelmsford reforms'. More people were now able to vote in elections for the central assembly and the provincial councils, and these bodies had more power. Congress should get its supporters elected to them so as to obstruct their work from within.

At first this idea was rejected. But those who favoured it went ahead and set up a *Swaraj* ('self-rule') Party, as part of Congress, to fight the elections. In 1924 they got many members into the councils. But the argument went on inside Congress for three years. The next set of reforms, in 1935, produced the same kind of argument.

Playing the game

These arguments, like the non-co-operation movement, were very typical of India and of British rule there. Though Gandhi had brought the common people into the struggle, none of the nationalists wanted a violent revolution or a guerrilla war. The struggle was more like a kind of game, whose rules were made by the British. So long as they did not break the rules, the nationalists were free to oppose the government. If they went too far, the government would use force against them.

Basically, each side respected the other, and expected it to stick to the rules. The nationalists *could* have launched a bloody rebellion. The British *could* have simply shot down demonstrators or kept all the nationalists permanently in prison. But neither side did so. The arguments between the British and Congress, or within Congress, all took 'the rules of the game' for granted.

Compare that with what happened in China (see chapters 9 and 11). Mao Tse-tung, China's great communist leader, said 'Power grows out of the barrel of a gun.' Gandhi said 'Non-violence.'

Jawaharlal Nehru

About this time, a new Congress leader came into prominence: Jawaharlal Nehru (1889–1964), Motilal Nehru's son. He was later to become India's first Prime Minister and the national leader.

He had been educated in England, but when he went back to India he threw himself into the national struggle, and was soon imprisoned. He became an admirer and close friend of Gandhi. But he was quite a different sort of man. He was very much 'westernized', like his father. He was not interested in religion.

Later he became a socialist. It was because of him that Congress stopped thinking only of equality between Indians and British and began to think seriously about getting equality between rich Indians and poor.

Nehru was – and remained throughout his life – the Congress leader most interested in international affairs. He saw that India's struggle for freedom was only part of a world-wide struggle against the colonial powers.

Dominion status or independence?

Nehru took a leading part in a new argument inside Congress.

The Swarajists had not simply been obstructive in the councils. They had argued, and begged the British to give India self-government, even if Britain still kept some powers in India. The British refused, and the Swarajists in 1926 walked out of the councils.

The mass movement had failed in 1922. Joining the councils had failed. What was to be done now? The young Congressmen, led by Nehru, argued that they should stop 'playing ball' with the British. They should demand complete independence for India without any links with Britain. The furthest Congress had gone so far was to demand 'Dominion status', which would leave India independent but still part of the British Empire, like Canada or Australia. The older men, among them Gandhi and Nehru's father Motilal, still supported this; young Nehru said it would tie India to British capitalism and Britain's 'reactionary' foreign policy.

The British played into Nehru's hands. They infuriated Indians by setting up a commission in 1927 to see what should be done next to make India's government more democratic – but without a single Indian member on the commission. Congress refused to have anything to do with it, and angrily passed a resolution calling for complete independence.

Gandhi and the elder Nehru hit back. With other political parties, a Congress committee, headed by the elder Nehru, drew up a report – the '[Motilal] Nehru report' – in favour of Dominion status. Young Nehru denounced it, and asked for a new campaign of non-co-operation.

At this point, British home politics took a hand. Britain in 1929 elected a Labour government. Congress was hopeful, and still more so when the Viceroy (the chief British official in India) declared that Dominion Status was Britain's goal for India and there would be a conference to work out the details.

But Britain's Labour government and the Viceroy soon started back-pedalling. Congress therefore refused to attend any conference. At the end of 1929 a meeting of Congress leaders again voted for complete independence and announced a new non-co-operation campaign.

This looked like a victory for Nehru and the young Congressmen. It was actually a victory for Gandhi, the great compromiser. He persuaded the meeting to vote against defining 'complete independence' as meaning a complete end to any connection with Britain, and Nehru accepted this.

So the way to future friendship between Britain and an independent India was left open. And once again Congress had chosen moderation instead of extremism.

Gandhi's salt march

Things looked different at the time, though. The new campaign of civil disobedience was launched. Again it was led by

Gandhi. This time he decided to break the law by making salt from sea-water without paying the salt tax.

His clever friends thought this absurd. But again Gandhi was right. The salt tax hit the poor people hardest. As Gandhi and his followers walked 240 miles from his home to the sea, their progress was reported in the newspapers and discussed all over India. Salt became the symbol of freedom.

The police were very tough in suppressing the new campaign. By midsummer of 1930, 60,000 Congress supporters were in prison.

But in 1931 Gandhi met the Viceroy and agreed to call the campaign off. That seemed to be to the disadvantage of Con-

6. *Congress supporters demonstrate with black flags against the commission headed by Sir John Simon that was set up in 1927 to suggest government reforms for India*

gress, but it was not. For the first time the British had, in effect, treated Congress as an equal.

More talks with the British followed, and then a new campaign of civil disobedience. Again many leaders, Gandhi and Nehru among them, were arrested. Gandhi at this moment turned his attention away from the British to his own campaign on behalf of the untouchables. He called off the civil disobedience.

Just as in 1922, other Congressmen were appalled. But they did not do anything. They knew that Gandhi was the one man who could inspire the Indian people. No Congress politician dared openly to oppose him.

7. THE ROAD TO PAKISTAN

The Government of India Act

In 1935, a new scheme for governing India (the Government of India Act, 1935) was announced. It was far more democratic than anything before. Though British officials would still control the central government, in the provinces there would be representative government. The number of people allowed to vote had been greatly increased: under the 'Morley-Minto reforms' of 1909, it had been about 30,000; under the 'Montagu-Chelmsford reforms' of 1919, about 6 million; after 1935 it was about 40 million. This act was based on the report of the Simon commission.

Congress against the Muslim League

But now the political struggle in India suddenly changed. From now on, the chief struggle was not between Congress and the British but between Congress and the Muslim League. The nearer India came to democracy, the more alarmed the Muslims became.

Since 1924 there had been many riots between Hindus and Muslims. In 1930 M. A. Jinnah (see chapter 4) and the Muslim League denounced the 'Nehru report' because its authors refused to allow for separate Muslim electorates voting for Muslim members.

In 1934, after three years in political retirement, Jinnah came back and reorganized the Muslim League. A year earlier a young Muslim, a student at Cambridge, had invented a name for a grouping of Indian provinces where Muslims were in a majority: Pakistan.

Congress makes a mistake

The new reforms gave Jinnah his chance. Congress had never liked the idea of separate electorates for the minorities. Nor did it like the Muslim League. It claimed to be *the* national party. It had a number of Muslim members. It argued that they, *as Congressmen,* would represent the Muslims.

The new reforms did give separate seats for the Muslims. The Congress leaders, after some arguing, had decided to take part in the elections, and were ready to form governments in the provinces where they did well. In the elections of 1936 they did even better than they had expected.

But they made one fatal mistake. In one province, Congress and the Muslim League had fought the elections as allies. The League expected to join Congress in forming a coalition government. Instead Congress said that any Muslim League member included in the government must quit the League and join Congress.

Congressmen thought this was perfectly reasonable: theirs was the national party. But the Muslim Leaguers were furious. They also complained that the new Congress governments were unfair to Muslims. Jinnah, a middle-class lawyer, decided that, like the Congress leaders, he too would appeal to the masses – the Muslim masses. And he succeeded. The Muslim League became the main party for the Muslims.

Whatever the British had done before, it was Congress itself in 1937–39 that divided Muslims from Hindus and so caused India eventually to be divided into two countries.

8. CHINA AND THE EUROPEANS

Europeans reach China

The first Westerners to reach China were merchants and missionaries, just as in India. But in China the results were different, because China was very different.

For many centuries, China was the heart of a great empire, whose borders spread far beyond the borders of China today. The whole country was ruled by an emperor through a well-organized civil service. In art, science and literature, the Chinese, until about 1500, could be regarded as in advance of the Europeans. They were proud of their culture, and regarded other people as barbarians.

So the first European merchants were treated as inferiors and kept in their place. Christian missionaries were closely controlled. After about 1750, there were few missionaries, and trade was allowed through only one port, Canton, in south China, and that under strict conditions.

The Westerners could not do what they did in India, and play off one native prince against another: there was only the emperor, the imperial court and the civil service to deal with. For the same reason they did not spread outside their trading posts and acquire territory of their own.

The Opium War

But in 1839 everything was changed by a war (the Opium War) with the British. The British wanted greater freedom to trade with China, particularly in the opium that was then grown in India. And they wanted to be treated as equals.

To the amazement of the Chinese, a small British force defeated the Chinese forces. The war ended in a treaty which gave the British a much better position.

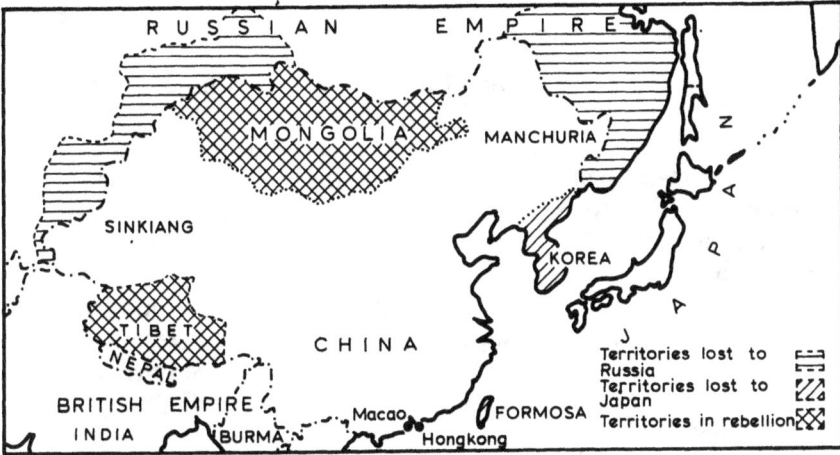

2. *China in 1914*

3. *Foreign encroachment on China*

The 'unequal treaties'

This was the first of a string of treaties that the Chinese were forced to sign with various European countries, the United States and Japan. The Chinese called them 'unequal treaties'. Their effect was to make the Chinese no longer masters in their own house. They were compelled to open their ports to foreign traders, and to allow foreign settlements, within the port areas, that were entirely controlled by foreigners.

By 1900 the great Chinese empire was like an aged lion torn to pieces by dogs. Russia, Japan, France, Britain and Germany each had carved out 'spheres of influence' in large parts of China, where they could do almost what they liked. Though the Chinese government was still supposed to be in charge, these spheres of influence were only one step away from being colonies pure and simple. The foreign trade, and the ports, railways and mines that the foreigners developed in their spheres of influence were, in fact, the first steps toward making China a modern country. But to Chinese at the time they seemed to be only a way of enriching the foreigners at China's expense.

Meanwhile the Chinese government had been forced to allow Christian missionaries to work, not only in the 'treaty ports' but in other parts of China. Their ideas offended the Chinese.

The Chinese were angry at what was happening to their country. In 1899 there was an anti-foreign and anti-Christian uprising (the Boxer Rebellion), which the imperial court supported. The uprising was defeated by foreign troops, and in the peace treaty that followed China was humiliated still further.

Sun Yat-sen

But meanwhile there were people in China and outside who began to ask why their country was being reduced to this wretched state. Some thought that all that was needed was to study the science and the military methods of the foreigners. Some thought the government system must be reformed as well.

But one man went much further. Sun Yat-sen (1866–1925) had received a Western education outside China. He reckoned that merely taking up Western ideas, or reforming the system of government, would never be enough. There must be a complete change from the top. Sun Yat-sen was determined to overthrow the emperor and have a parliamentary government instead. He formed secret societies among Chinese living overseas and planned revolution.

Inside China, the increasing number of students who had come back after being educated abroad spread the same ideas. Support for the imperial family grew steadily less.

The revolution

In 1911, after several unsuccessful attempts, a rebellion broke out in south China. Leaders of various revolutionary groups met in Nanking and proclaimed 'the Republic of China'. Sun Yat-sen, who was in the United States, came back and was proclaimed president.

7. *1912. Recruiting for the revolution. The flags are those of the Kuomintang, blue with a white many-pointed star*

But northern China was still to be won. There the imperial government had appointed Yuan Shih-kai (1859–1916) virtually dictator, with power to crush the rebellion. Instead he negotiated with Sun Yat-sen.

The emperor Pu Yi, a young boy (he still lives peacefully today in communist China) was forced to abdicate. The Empire was at an end.

In return Yuan Shih-kai was appointed president of the republic in Sun's place. It soon became clear, however, that what he really wanted was to become emperor himself.

When elections for a parliament were held in 1913, Sun Yat-sen's party, the Kuomintang, did best. But Yuan Shih-kai had the party leader, Sun's chief supporter, murdered. The Kuomintang organized a revolt against him, but he defeated it, dissolved parliament and outlawed the Kuomintang.

In 1915 Yuan announced that he would become emperor. But there were new rebellions against him, in south China, and foreign countries opposed him. Yuan had to withdraw his plan, and in 1916 he died.

The 'warlords'

The republic and the parliamentary constitution were restored. But in fact Yuan had killed them. The Kuomintang soon withdrew from the Peking government in north China, and set up one of its own at Canton in the south.

For the next ten years the Peking government was a joke. The real power in China was held by the 'warlords', men who controlled the various provinces or regions. Some were army officers, one or two former civil servants, others simply bandits who had fought their way to the top. Each controlled his own area by force, and tried to extend his control by alliances with other warlords, or by war against them. Each hoped that in the end he might seize control of all China.

9. THE RISE OF
THE KUOMINTANG

Why democracy failed

The first experiment in Western-style democracy in China had failed, and it was never tried again. It failed (contrast this with India) because it was introduced far too quickly in a country that was unaccustomed to any kind of democratic behaviour. The Chinese knew nothing about free speech, a free press, tolerance of disagreement, and other principles that make a democratic system possible. Nor did they have what was equally important, a single, strong government.

Sun Yat-sen's three principles

Sun Yat-sen came to realize, during the years when the war-lords ruled China, that it was no use just to imitate the Western system. Instead he proposed what he called 'the three principles of the people'. These were:

1. *Nationalism,* which meant getting rid of foreign interference.

2. *Democracy,* which Sun saw only as the last of three stages. First, the Kuomintang would unify China by force; second, while still keeping power itself, it would train the people for self-government; third, eventually a fully democratic government would be set up.

3. *People's Livelihood,* a vague expression which meant, roughly, that no one was to be allowed to have too much land or become too rich.

The second and third principles had little effect at the time, though the Kuomintang government on Formosa (see chapter 15) now claims to follow them. But the first principle, nationalism, was a different story.

Foreign interference goes on

It was natural that nationalism was Sun's first principle. There was still great feeling against foreigners in China at this time. The Japanese and Europeans had not given up their interference in China. Indeed, the weakness of the Chinese after 1911 encouraged them still further. For instance:

1. The British encouraged Tibet, which was part of the Chinese Empire but had rebelled in 1912 and had proclaimed itself independent. In 1914 the (British) Indian government made an agreement – the Simla Convention – with the Tibetans. They drew on a map a frontier between Tibet and China. In return, the Tibetans allowed the British to draw a new border (the McMahon Line) between Tibet and north-eastern India which was in India's favour. Though a Chinese diplomat had attended part of the conference, China would not accept its results (see chapter 24).

2. Outer Mongolia, also part of the Chinese Empire, fell more and more under Russian influence. Eventually it became altogether independent. Today, still under Russian influence, it is called the Mongolian People's Republic.

3. Japan had already seized the island of Formosa, which was part of China, in 1895, and Korea, which had been under Chinese control, in 1910. After 1914, during the First World War, the Japanese took everything the Germans had held in China and demanded even more (for a fuller story, see chapter 10).

The 'May 4th incident'

When the world war ended, the victorious Allies abolished some of the concessions China had made to Germany. But the Japanese were allowed to keep the former German 'rights' in Shantung. This set off student demonstrations in Peking on May 4, 1919, against the Japanese and the Europeans who were ready to give way to them.

At a conference held in Washington in 1921–22, something was done to give China back its rights. The Japanese agreed to withdraw from Shantung. It was agreed that no foreign country would try to get a special position for itself in China (this was mainly aimed at Russia and Japan) and that all countries wished China to remain united.

The 'May 30th movement'

But there were still other things for Chinese to feel angry about. Foreigners held the top jobs in the customs service, and the entire customs duties went directly to pay China's debts to foreigners. The 'treaty port' of Shanghai was virtually run by foreigners – there were even public parks there from which Chinese were kept out. In many 'treaty ports' – ports opened to foreigners under the 'unequal treaties' – the foreigners had special privileges. They had 'extra-territorial rights', meaning they were subject to the law of their own countries and not to Chinese law.

At the Washington conference it had been promised that these grievances would be looked into. But by 1925 little had been done.

On May 30th in that year, British-officered police killed thirteen Chinese demonstrators in Shanghai. A little later, British and French troops killed fifty at Canton. There was tremendous anger in China. Goods from Hong Kong (a British colony on the south coast of China) were boycotted, and Chinese factory workers there went on strike.

The 'New Culture movement'

Along with anti-foreign feeling there came a tremendous spread of new ideas in China. All sorts of old Chinese traditions were attacked. Students debated about religion and such traditional Chinese virtues as loyalty to the state and obedience to one's parents. Writers began to start using the ordinary spoken language instead of the elaborate literary language which only well-educated people could understand.

This 'New Culture movement' arose out of the May 4th incident and was most vigorous from 1919 to 1921. It was partly anti-foreign but (unlike the Boxer Rebellion of 1899, for instance) it was not directed against foreign *ideas*. On the contrary, exactly because they wanted to modernize China the reformers were eager to make use of modern ideas from the West.

The growth of communism

One idea that was growing in Europe at the time was communism. It began to attract educated Chinese soon after the

Russian Revolution of 1917. Communist ideas about imperialism seemed to explain very well what had happened in China in the last eighty years. Then came the May 4th incident. The students were in a mood of angry nationalism. Communist ideas began to spread among them, particularly when the new communist government of Russia announced that it (unlike Britain, France, Japan or America) would give up any claims over China that had been gained through 'unequal treaties'.

In 1921 the first congress of the Communist Party of China was held. Among the first members were some who have become famous: Mao Tse-tung (born 1893); Chou En-lai (born 1898); Chen Yi (born 1901). In 1967 these men were respectively Chairman of the Party, Prime Minister, and Foreign Minister of China.

The communists join the Kuomintang

In 1922, the communists offered to co-operate with the Kuomintang as equals, although the Communist Party was much smaller. Sun Yat-sen would not accept that, but he was ready to let them join his party while remaining members of their own. Already he had seen how much the communists in Russia had gained by having a well-organized and disciplined party which kept the power of the state in its own hands; and, some months after the May 4th incident, he had begun to reorganize the Kuomintang on that pattern. He saw that the Chinese communists could help him. The Russians persuaded the Chinese communists to do so, and themselves offered the Kuomintang Russian help and advice.

Sun Yat-sen agreed, and soon many Russian advisers were sent to help the Kuomintang organize their party and to train a party army for it. Sun sent his chief soldier to Russia to study Russian methods. This was General Chiang Kai-shek (born 1887). When he came back he set up a military academy in China, whose chief political instructor was the communist Chou En-lai.

Later the communists and the Kuomintang became deadly enemies, and are so today. Yet the Kuomintang might never have come to anything without the support of the Russians and the skill of the Chinese communists. Sun Yat-sen's 'three principles' were no more than hopeful ideas, whereas the communists gave the Kuomintang discipline and force.

The alliance breaks up

For a time the communist-Kuomintang alliance worked. But strains soon began to show after Sun Yat-sen's death in early 1925. The right-wing Kuomintang leaders, headed by Chiang Kai-shek, began to fear the growing strength of the communists both inside the Kuomintang organization and in student movements and trade unions. In 1926 Chiang Kai-shek dismissed some of the communist leaders at Canton, the Kuomintang base, and sent Russian military advisers home.

For the time being, though, the alliance held together. Later in 1926, the 'Northern Expedition' began. Till now the power of the Kuomintang had been confined to southern China, round Canton. The supposed government of China was still in Peking in the north. Sun Yat-sen had planned a great military drive northwards to unify China. This was it.

It was a huge success. The army, and the nationalist propagandists who went with it, were welcomed. Many of the warlords joined Chiang with their troops. By the end of 1926, much of southern China up to the Yangtze valley had been won over.

But now trouble began. While Chiang's army was fighting, the Kuomintang government, which had moved to Wuhan, came more and more under left-wing influence. Chiang was alarmed. In 1927, having entered Shanghai with the active help of the communists there, among them Chou En-lai, he suddenly turned on the communists. Thousands were slaughtered.

Chiang now set up a rival government at Nanking. The Wuhan government disowned him. But when the communists there tried to organize a mass movement against Chiang, the Kuomintang leaders became alarmed. They too turned on the communists, and defeated them (for what happened later, see chapter 11).

The leaders from Wuhan now joined Chiang. In 1928 he marched north again and captured Peking (though Nanking remained the capital city). Foreign countries now recognized the Nanking government as the government of China. The country was at last more or less united – or so it seemed.

Chiang's enemies

In the next three years Chiang Kai-shek managed to get rid of many of the privileges of the European powers. But he had to face two enemies who eventually destroyed his power: the Chinese communists and the Japanese imperialists.

10. JAPAN SEIZES AN EMPIRE

Japan keeps out the Europeans

Of the three great Asian countries, only Japan managed to remain completely independent of the European empires. The Japanese did it by keeping the foreigners out. For about fifty years Portuguese merchants and missionaries were active and many Japanese were converted to Christianity. But, after a rebellion by Christian Japanese in 1637, all Europeans were banned, while Japanese were forbidden to leave Japan.

For two centuries, the Japanese were completely cut off from Europeans, except for a few Dutch merchants. However, in the 1850s, first the Americans, then the Russians and British, forced the Japanese to open their ports to trade. Treaties were signed which allowed Japan to charge only low customs duties and gave foreigners 'extra-territorial' rights, just as in China.

Modernizing Japan

The Japanese resented these treaties. But unlike the Chinese they set to work, under the emperor Meiji, to modernize their own country so that it would be the equal of any other. In the next fifty years Japan was totally transformed from an old-fashioned country into a modern one with railways, industries, shipbuilding yards, schools, universities, and a modern army.

In 1889 a modern constitution was introduced under which there was to be a kind of parliament elected by a small rich minority. Political parties had already been set up.

But Japan did not develop in a democratic way. In the period before 1900 several things happened which made an immense difference to the course of Japanese history up till 1945.

1. For centuries, the real power in Japan had not been the emperor but the *shogun,* an official belonging to a particular clan. In 1867, this system was ended by the 'Meiji Restoration' and thereafter everything was done to create loyalty to the emperor. He was treated almost as if he were a god. The Shinto religion, the ancient religion of Japan, dating from the mythical days of the first Japanese emperor, was used to encourage this idea.

2. The government, determined to modernize Japan as fast as possible, had set up many industries. But later these were sold to a few private companies, called the *zaibatsu.* These companies and the families controlling them became immensely rich. The *zaibatsu* in turn did much to modernize Japan. But they were very ruthless, and they had a harmful effect on politics; many politicians were bribed by them.

3. It became the custom that the army and navy ministers in the government should always be serving officers. This gave the armed forces great power, since they could always refuse to supply a minister to some prime minister of whom they disapproved.

Aggression and empire-building

The Japanese were determined to get rid of the 'unequal treaties' that had been forced on them. By 1900 they had more or less succeeded.

But they also wanted more. They wanted Japan to become a great power, which meant expanding its influence over its neighbours. For over fifty years (1894–1945) Japan steadily, and ruthlessly, expanded its Empire, mainly at China's expense, as follows:

1. *1894–95.* War with China over Korea, a Chinese protectorate. The Japanese won and the peace treaty gave them Formosa and the Liaotung peninsula. Joint pressure from France, Germany and Russia forced them to give up the Liaotung peninsula. Three years later Russia 'leased' it from China.

2. *1904–05.* War with Russia, again over Korea. Again Japan won – the first time an Asian nation had defeated a European one. Japan got Russia's lease of the Liaotung

peninsula and its railway in southern Manchuria (part of China).

3. *1907.* A secret treaty with Russia divided Manchuria into Japanese and Russian 'spheres of influence'.

4. *1910.* Korea, already under Japan's thumb, was annexed as a colony.

5. *1912.* Russia and Japan agreed to divide Inner Mongolia (part of China) into 'spheres of influence'. The British and the Americans meanwhile did nothing to stop them.

6. *1914.* When the First World War broke out, the Japanese joined in against the Germans so that they could seize the German 'leased' territory and all German rights in Shantung.

7. *1915.* A list of twenty-one demands was made to China that would have made it just a puppet of Japan. The Chinese (Yuan Shih-kai) refused the worst ones, but had to agree to Japan keeping what it had taken from Germany. It was the Allies' willingness to let Japan keep this at the end of the war that led to China's 'May 4th movement' (see chapter 9).

But Japan seemed to have changed its ways at the Washington conference (see chapter 9). It gave up some of what it had taken. And for several years after that, there was peace.

The collapse of democracy

This peace ended because the semi-democratic system in Japan broke down.

From 1889 until the death of the emperor Meiji in 1912, the political parties were growing in importance. But all the time, the small group of 'elder statesmen' – the men who had carried out the Meiji Restoration – were there to keep them under control and to see that nothing was changed too fast.

In the First World War, Japan became rich as all the Allied nations ordered war materials from it. The numbers of factories, and of people working in them, almost doubled in the four years 1914–18. As in England, this led to the growth both of socialist ideas (which the government tried to suppress) and of more simply democratic ones. Meanwhile the 'elder statesmen' were, literally, dying off.

After the war ended, Japan seemed to be moving towards normal party politics. But three things prevented this:

1. The more powerful the civilian politicians became, the

more alarmed the army and navy officers became that their own importance would grow less. For instance, in 1924 the government decided to cut down the size of the army very sharply.

2. In 1927 there was a financial crisis in Japan. Many banks and companies went bankrupt. The huge *zaibatsu* companies survived and indeed did well by buying up bankrupt factories cheaply. This made people distrust the *zaibatsu*.

3. The politicians were corrupt. Many were bribed by the *zaibatsu* and still more were believed to be.

The growth of militarism

When the world-wide slump of 1929–30 hit Japan, all these things combined to make people feel that the democratic system had failed and that some tougher kind of government was needed. In the army, many young officers felt that 'these civilians are ruining Japan'. The same people were indignant at what they thought was the 'soft' attitude of the civilian governments toward China. They believed that Japan, a strong country, had the right to take what it could from China, a weak one.

One person who opposed this was the emperor Hirohito, who came to the throne in 1926. But he could do nothing: although the emperor was all-powerful in theory, in fact he had to do what the government told him. And the people's loyalty to the *emperor* was used to make it seem 'disloyal' to criticize the *government*.

The Japanese army attacks China

In 1931 the Japanese army – without any orders from the government – started a war with China. There had already been clashes during Chiang Kai-shek's Northern Expedition. Japan had sent troops into Shantung in 1928 to block his advance, and a few months later some Japanese officers murdered the Chinese warlord of Manchuria, as part of a plot to seize Manchuria. But then their senior officers did not back them up.

But in 1931 an army plot was cooked up. Japanese troops seized the Manchurian city of Mukden, and soon had taken most of Manchuria, which was later turned into an 'independent' – i.e. Japanese-run – state and called Manchukuo. In 1932, Chinese troops in Shanghai were attacked.

The Japanese government could do nothing about it: the army was out of control. A new Prime Minister was appointed, who tried to bring the soldiers to heel. He was murdered within a few months. That was the end of government by party politicians in Japan until 1945.

From now on the army took more and more power, and the government could do little but give way for fear of being overthrown altogether. Indeed in 1936 some young officers, with 1,500 men, tried to seize power in Tokyo, and murdered several important politicians. Though they failed, Japan was now almost a military state. 'Patriotism' was taught in the schools, and all other ideas, liberal, socialist or communist, were suppressed.

11. WAR IN CHINA

Chiang against the communists

In China, the Japanese War did not at first greatly affect Chiang Kai-shek's government at Nanking. Chiang was busy trying to unite China. That meant getting rid of foreigners and their 'spheres of influence' and 'extra-territorial rights'. In this he was generally successful; indeed it was his efforts to restore Chinese control in Manchuria that led to the Japanese attack.

Chiang's main efforts were spent on military campaigns against various warlords, and against the Chinese communists. Between 1931 and 1934 he launched five campaigns against the communists.

The communists had been routed in 1927 by the Kuomintang troops (see chapter 9). In Canton and another city they had tried to launch rebellions, and been crushed. Mao Tse-tung had tried a rebellion among the peasants of southern China, and that was crushed too. The communists were driven into Kiangsi province, where they set up a 'soviet' – a communist government – led by Mao and Chu Teh, a former warlord.

Town or countryside?

There was soon a dispute inside the Communist Party about the way to win power. Mao Tse-tung believed that in China the backbone of any revolution must be the peasants in the countryside. The national party leader, Li Li-san, believed it must be the industrial workers in the towns. So did the Comintern, the international communist organization run from Moscow by the Russians.

Events proved Mao right. When the communists tried mass

uprisings in certain towns, the Kuomintang soldiers suppressed them by force. When communist troops seized one town, the Kuomintang army came and threw them out.

The Comintern – which greatly influenced the Chinese Communist Party – decided to get rid of Li Li-san. But they kept on his chief helper, Chou En-lai. He and a group known as the 'returned students' – Chinese who had studied communism in Russia – took over the party. They still believed in Li Li-san's ideas. By now the national party leaders had moved to Kiangsi, and they began to take control of Mao's 'soviet'.

The 'Long March'

But, unintentionally, Chiang Kai-shek saved Mao. The fifth anti-communist campaign, in 1934, was fiercer than all the others. Kiangsi was blockaded. The communists had to choose between being squeezed into surrender, or abandoning Kiangsi.

They decided to break out. In October 1934, the 'Long March' began. For a year the communist army and its followers – possibly 100,000 people in all – marched westward and then north. It covered 6,000 miles, eighteen mountain ranges, twenty-four major rivers. All the time it was under attack. But after this immense journey, the 30,000 who were left found safety in Yenan, in Shensi province, part of northwest China near the Soviet Union.

By then Mao Tse-tung was firmly in command. Possibly because they were incompetent soldiers, the 'returned students' had lost the confidence of their followers. From now on, Mao, with his belief in countryside revolution, not city revolution, and in guerrilla warfare, not ordinary warfare, was the political and military leader of the Chinese communists.

The Sian incident

All this time, Chiang Kai-shek had avoided open war with the Japanese. He now tried to attack the communists in their new stronghold at Shensi. But the government soldiers in the north were unwilling to fight. When, in December 1936, Chiang flew up to see that the anti-communist campaign was pushed ahead, he was seized and held prisoner at a place called Sian by his own troops. They demanded that he should stop fighting the Chinese communists and start fighting China's real enemy, the Japanese.

Some communist leaders, led by Chou En-lai, arrived at Sian. The Comintern wanted China united, to fight Japan. So, unwillingly, the Chinese communist leaders agreed to form a united front with the Kuomintang. Chiang was forced to agree and was then released. He and Chou En-lai went back to Nanking.

China fights Japan

The real war against Japan now began. The Japanese were alarmed to see the Chinese uniting against them. They organized a clash with Chinese troops near Peking (the Marco Polo Bridge incident) and in mid 1937 launched a full-scale war.

The war against Japan was to last from 1937 to 1945. The Japanese soon overran most of north-east China. They then attacked in the Yangtze valley. They captured Shanghai, then

8. *Japanese armoured cars enter Shanghai*

Nanking. The Chinese government fled, first to Wuhan, then in late 1938 to Chungking in the far west of China. The Japanese meanwhile had taken Canton, in the south.

For the rest of the war they occupied the Chinese coastal areas and all the important towns and road and rail routes in eastern China. In Nanking they set up a puppet government.

The communists grow strong

Chiang Kai-shek had fought skilfully. He received weapons and supplies from the Russians, British and Americans. But throughout the war his government became steadily weaker compared with the communists.

The communists in Shensi had concentrated on winning over the peasants, but without being very violent against the landlords; for instance, they generally reduced rents rather than confiscating the land and giving it to the tenant-farmers.

Under the united front agreement of 1937, they promised to make their army part of the national Chinese army, and to put their government under central government control. They said they would stop anti-Kuomintang propaganda and actions against landlords.

They did not keep their promises. Their army, now called the Eighth Route Army, spread over much of northern China. Everywhere it went, political agitators went with it, teaching the peasants communism. Its resistance to the Japanese won the support of many patriotic Chinese for communism.

Under Mao Tse-tung's leadership, the army developed the art of guerrilla war. In many areas behind the Japanese lines, communist guerrillas operated successfully. They even set up governments in these areas. They fought the Japanese, but they also fought Kuomintang troops, and killed anti-communists among the peasants.

The Kuomintang grows weaker

On his side, Chiang, from about 1941, was just as busy fighting the communists as fighting the Japanese. His government at this time became more and more oppressive and corrupt. In far-away Chungking, the landlords who supported the Kuomintang became more influential. The Chungking government could not match the communists' appeal to the ordinary peasants. In the towns, prices rose and the millions of people who had fled from eastern China lived in misery.

The government also had to fight the war. It is often said that the communists provided the only real resistance to the Japanese. That is untrue. The money and effort spent on fighting Japan would have been spent better in improving the life of the Chinese people. But that was out of the question.

12. THE SECOND WORLD
WAR BEGINS

Politics in India

In September 1939, the Second World War began in Europe.
The only immediate effect in Asia was a political crisis in
India.

9. *Congress leaders meet in 1940. The photograph shows two of the
   top three – Gandhi (centre) and Vallabhbhai Patel (middle left) –
   and was taken by the third, Nehru himself. His sister Vijaylakshmi,
   also an active politician, is in the background*

There, the British Viceroy at once declared that India was at war too, without consulting Congress leaders. The eight Congress provincial governments (see chapter 7) resigned in protest.

They had been doing some useful things – and building Congress power. Now they went back to futile opposition. The Muslim League was delighted. In the parts of India where Muslims were in a majority, provincial governments loyal to the League carried on. The League strengthened its hold on the Muslim masses.

In early 1940, at a national conference, the League passed the 'Pakistan resolution' demanding that Muslim areas in eastern and north-western India should form 'independent states'. At the time, no one was very clear what that meant. But it led eventually to the creation of Pakistan.

Meanwhile, Congress opposed the British war effort. On conditions (which the British refused) they would support the war, they said. But though Nehru, for one, hated Nazism, they did not see why Indians should fight to preserve the British Empire.

Yet many Indians did so. Large numbers joined the Indian army and fought on Britain's side. (Until the 1960s most senior Indian and Pakistani officers were men who fought well in the Second World War.) But in India thousands of Congress members were jailed in 1940–41 for acts of civil disobedience, after Congress had rejected a British offer of independence *after* the war in return for co-operation at once.

Japan looks south

In 1940, the European war began to have effects on Japan. Japan's attack on China, and its bombing of civilian targets, had angered the Americans. America was arming Chiang Kai-shek, and in 1940 began to cut down deliveries to Japan of oil and supplies that might be used for war.

In 1940, the Germans won great victories against Britain and France. This made the Americans more eager for a settlement with Japan, since (though still neutral) they regarded Germany as 'enemy number one'. But it encouraged the Japanese to think of moving southwards into the British, French and Dutch colonies. They rightly reckoned that these

countries were too weak now to defend their colonies –
(British) Malaya, French Indochina, and the Dutch East
Indies (now Indonesia).

The Japanese had no oil supplies of their own. They
wanted the oil of the Dutch East Indies, and the rubber of
Malaya. They also wanted to stop supplies reaching Chiang
Kai-shek through Burma, which the British controlled, and
through Indochina. Both Britain and France gave way on
that, and the French even allowed Japanese troops into
Indochina.

The road to war

The first steps to a Japanese-American war came in September
1940. Japan, Germany and Italy agreed that if America
attacked any of them, the others would come to its help. At
the same time, the Americans, alarmed by Japanese troop
movements into Indochina banned all sales of scrap steel,
vital for Japan's war industries, to them.

But neither country wanted war. In early 1941 they began
talks. The Americans wanted Japan to withdraw its troops
from China and Indochina. The Japanese were determined to
keep troops at least in northern China; for protection against
communism, they said.

In mid 1941, the Americans discovered (from messages in
a secret Japanese code which they had learned to decipher)
that the Japanese were preparing to occupy still more of
Indochina. America, Britain and Holland 'froze' all Japanese
money in their banks, and cut off all oil supplies.

The Japanese were now forced to choose. Either they must
reach agreement with America before their oil stocks ran out,
or they must seize the oil of the Dutch East Indies. The Prime
Minister was ready to give in further to the Americans to reach
an agreement. The army was not. The Prime Minister resigned,
and the army leader General Hideki Tojo took his place. The
talks with the Americans dragged on, but at the end of
November 1941 they broke down completely. War was now
certain.

The Americans did not want to strike first, but they were
quite willing to provoke Japan into doing so. But they did not
foresee how Japan would strike.

Pearl Harbor

At dawn on December 7, 1941, aircraft from Japanese carriers, sent out beforehand into the Pacific Ocean, bombed the American fleet stationed at Pearl Harbor in Hawaii. The fleet was taken completely by surprise. Five battleships were sunk, two more seriously damaged. Most of the American planes were destroyed on the ground.

Japanese bombers from Formosa did the same to American planes at Manila in the Philippine Islands. Japanese troops landed by night in Malaya and attacked the great British base at Singapore. Two British battleships were sunk at sea by planes.

Within three days most of the British and American strength in the Pacific had been destroyed.

Who was to blame?

It is often believed that Pearl Harbor was a treacherous attack that came completely without warning.

Yet only a few months before, American commanders in Hawaii had prepared a defence plan anticipating just this kind of attack. When the Americans learned on December 6th, from Japanese code messages, that Japan's last message to them was to be delivered at one o'clock next day in Washington, one American colonel pointed out that that would be dawn – the ideal hour for attack – in Hawaii. A warning was actually sent to Hawaii, but by commercial cable lines. It arrived as the bombs were falling.

In any case the Americans knew the war was coming within a few days. And, though the real fault was Japan's for attacking China, it was a war that America had helped to provoke.

13. JAPAN LOSES THE WAR

Victory — and defeat

At first, the Japanese had complete success. Within seven months they had captured Hong Kong, Malaya and Singapore, the Dutch East Indies, Burma, the Philippine Islands. It looked as if India and Australia would be invaded.

But in mid 1942 the Americans won a great naval victory, the Battle of Midway. In New Guinea, Australian and American troops halted the invading force and then destroyed it. American submarines were soon sinking many Japanese merchant ships – by early 1943 ten times as many as were being built.

From then on, the Japanese were gradually forced back. They fought with extraordinary bravery, but they could not match the immense sea and air power of the Americans. In 1944 they launched their last counter-attacks. They advanced successfully in south-west China. In Burma they tried to break through into India. But there they were utterly defeated.

In the Pacific Ocean the Americans were advancing, island by island, toward Japan. At Leyte Gulf, in the Philippines, in October 1944, virtually all that was left of the Japanese fleet was destroyed. It was only a matter of time – and of very bitter battles – before Japan would be defeated.

The end of the Western empires

But the Japanese, in one sense, were successful. They did not create a new Japanese empire for themselves, but they effectively destroyed the Western empires in Asia.

They claimed to be creating a 'Greater East Asia Co-prosperity Sphere' in which the 'liberated' Asians would co-operate. This propaganda was almost entirely dishonest:

the Japanese were actually after their own advantage. They were often very brutal, and they treated most of the genuine nationalists with contempt. But they had to make some allowance for nationalist feelings. They declared Burma and the Philippines 'independent', and as the war ended were about to do the same for the Dutch East Indies. They also deliberately humiliated captured Europeans, to destroy the idea that the white races were superior.

Their own brutality toward other Asians also led to the formation of nationalist resistance movements, for instance in Malaya. These were mainly communist-led and after Japan's defeat became anti-imperialist. In French Indochina, the Kuomintang Chinese backed a nationalist movement headed by Ho Chi Minh, who is today the communist leader of North Vietnam, and an ally of the Chinese communists.

The 'quit India' movement

The Japanese War also affected India. Alarmed by Japan's successes in early 1942, the British made a new offer to the Indian nationalists: independence after the war, and an all-party national government at once. But they still insisted that Britain must be in charge of India's defence. So Congress refused the offer. Congress also doubted Britain's sincerity; and anyway, they thought it would soon be the Japanese, not the British, that they would have to deal with. As Gandhi put it, why accept 'a postdated cheque on a failing bank'?

Instead Congress launched a 'quit India' campaign of sabotage and violence. The British firmly repressed it and arrested all the Congress leaders. Over 900 people were killed on both sides, and the railways were partly paralysed by sabotage. But, for all the enthusiasm it aroused, the campaign achieved nothing.

The Indian National Army

Now a former Congress leader reappeared: Subhas Chandra Bose, who had been one of the most extreme young Congressmen in the 1920s and who became Congress President in 1938 and 1939, but had fallen out with Gandhi. In danger of arrest by the British, he had fled in 1941 first to Russia, then to Germany, and finally to Japan.

With Japanese help he organized an 'Indian National Army' from among Indians captured at the fall of Singapore. There, in 1943, he proclaimed a 'free government of India', and in 1944 the INA took part in the Japanese attack in Burma. The attack, and with it the INA, was shattered. In 1945, just before Japan surrendered, Bose was killed in an aircrash.

But that was not the end of the story. After the war, the British foolishly put on trial three officers of the INA. By accident, they were the perfect symbols of a united India: a Hindu, a Muslim and a Sikh. Congress took up their cause, and the trial became a demonstration against British rule.

The war and China

For China, America's entry into the war had two effects. It meant that the Americans, instead of being friendly neutrals

10. *War against Japan. Chinese civilians sabotage a railway track. The picture, put out by the communist Chinese news agency, illustrates Mao Tse-tung's ideas on 'people's war'*

were now open allies. But the Japanese successes also meant that the Americans had little to spare for their allies and that it was harder to deliver, the land route through Burma being cut. Supplies had to be flown in to Chungking.

In early 1941, the united front of Kuomintang and communists had more or less collapsed, after Kuomintang troops attacked a communist army south of the Yangtze, where, they said, it had no right to be. From then on, both the communists and the Kuomintang were spending more and more of their effort on fighting each other rather than the Japanese.

The Americans basically backed the Kuomintang, but their first interest was in the war against Japan. They urged in 1944 that Chiang Kai-shek should give the communists a share in the government, and suggested that American aid should go direct to the communist forces, as well as the government. Chiang Kai-shek refused. He knew that once Japan was defeated by the United States, as it was bound to be, the struggle for control of China would break out openly.

China is sacrificed

The Americans not only cared more for defeating Japan than for helping Chiang Kai-shek, they were also ready to sacrifice China itself.

In 1945, Churchill, Stalin and Roosevelt, meeting at Yalta, agreed that the Russians would help to free China from Japan, and would make a treaty with Chiang Kai-shek's government. In return, after Japan's defeat, China would give the Russians the same (very considerable) rights in Manchuria as the Russian emperors had had in 1905, including the naval base of Port Arthur.

Chiang Kai-shek was in no position to resist, and in August 1945, he made a treaty on these terms. All he got in return was a promise that the Russians would give military aid only to his government and not to the communists.

The atomic bomb

In August 1945, the war was brought to a sudden end. The Japanese already were near defeat and were seeking peace. On July 26th, the Allies had called on them to surrender unconditionally or face 'prompt and utter destruction', but no attempt was made to explain what that meant.

On August 6th the Japanese found out. The first atomic bomb was dropped on the city of Hiroshima. In an instant the whole centre of the city was destroyed and 80,000 people were killed. Thousands more died of radiation sickness in the weeks and months afterwards. On August 9th, the second atomic bomb destroyed the city of Nagasaki. On August 15th, Japan surrendered.

At the time, and afterwards, the Allies justified their use of atomic bombs by saying that it had made an invasion of Japan unnecessary and saved hundreds of thousands of lives. But the Allies knew – at the time – that the Japanese were already looking for peace. Even if they had not been, could they not have been given warning to evacuate Hiroshima? Or could not the atomic bomb have been used on some little-inhabited place as a demonstration of its power?

No satisfactory answer to these questions has ever been given. Most Asians believe that the dropping of the first atomic bombs was an unjustifiable crime, and one that would never have been committed if Japan had been a European country. Japanese and most other Asians were left with a deep hatred of atomic weapons.

14. INDIA AND PAKISTAN

The British quit India

Japan had been crushed. Yet in fighting for entirely selfish reasons, the Japanese had liberated Asia. The British were exhausted. They no longer had the money, or the will, to hang on to distant parts of their Empire if they could get out honourably and without leaving chaos behind them. They also had a Labour government, elected in mid 1945. Unlike Churchill, the new Prime Minister, Clement Attlee, was happy enough to see the Empire break up. Within two years, India was free.

The partition of India

But it was partitioned. By 1945, the gap between Congress and the Muslim League had become unbridgeable. Elections in 1945 proved that Congress had the support of nearly all Hindus, but the Muslim League (unlike 1937) now had equally strong support among Muslims. The British and the Congress leaders tried endlessly to work out ways of making India free as a single country. Jinnah insisted that the Muslims must have a country of their own, Pakistan.

Attlee decided something must be done. In early 1947 he announced that, whatever happened, the British would quit by mid 1948. He sent out a new Viceroy, Lord Mountbatten, whose main job was to arrange the details.

At last the Congress leaders had to face the facts. Within a few months India would be governed by Indians, and the new government would be able to rely on no one's strength but its own. In the Muslim provinces it simply would not be able to govern. Unless they wanted chaos, they must accept Jinnah's terms. Sadly, they did.

In June 1947, Mountbatten announced a plan for the partition of India to which both Congress and the Muslim League had agreed. Because the British administration was already breaking down, he brought forward the date of independence. At midnight on August 14th, 1947, India and Pakistan went their separate ways, free.

Religious massacres

But they were not at peace. Unavoidably, the boundary-lines left many Muslims still living within India, many Hindus and Sikhs in Pakistan. It had been hoped that these minorities would be able to stay peacefully where they were. But in some areas, particularly in Punjab, which had been divided between

11. *1947. Britain hands over power. While Lord Mountbatten, the last Viceroy, listens, Jinnah addresses Pakistani leaders a few hours before their country becomes free*

India and Pakistan, they felt insecure. Refugees began to flee across the borders.

As they went, they were attacked by fanatics of the other religion. Muslims slaughtered Sikhs and Hindus; Sikhs and (less often) Hindus slaughtered Muslims. When the refugees reached safety across the border, their stories of horror led to further massacres in revenge. In both countries the governments tried to restrain their people, but could not. When the slaughter ended, 200,000 people had been killed, 7 million Muslims had fled to Pakistan, 4½ million Sikhs and Hindus had fled to India.

Today, some 50 million Muslims – about one-tenth of the Indian population – live in India. In West Pakistan only a tiny fraction of non-Muslims remains. In East Pakistan, where the violence was much less, there are about 10 million Hindus living among 50 million Muslims.

In both countries they live, usually, in peace. India's constitution promises equal rights to those of all religions (indeed, the present President is a Muslim). Pakistan is avowedly a Muslim country, and, though Hindus have the same political rights as anyone else there are few Hindus in public life. But in both countries there is always the fear that the enmity between the countries will be turned into enmity between the two religions, and that fanatics will turn on the helpless minorities in their midst.

The princes

Why is there still enmity between India and Pakistan? Mainly because the British made a terrible mistake in dealing with the Indian princes. There were nearly 600 of them. Some ruled states of a few square miles, others had many thousands of square miles. The British never ruled these states directly. They let the princes govern as they chose – some well, some very badly – merely insisting that the princes recognize the British as the 'paramount power', the people who in the last resort could decide what was to be done.

When they freed India, the British did not insist that the princes must now recognize the new governments of India and Pakistan as 'paramount'. They said the princes had the right to join whichever country they chose, or to remain inde-

pendent. This was correct in law, but impossible in practice.
It might have left India, in particular, looking like a patchwork
quilt, with independent states or even bits of Pakistan dotted
all over it.

The Kashmir dispute

That did not happen, because the new Indian government was
tough. It persuaded or bullied the princes whose states were
within its borders into joining India. But trouble arose over
Kashmir, a large state lying between India and Pakistan. The

4. *India and Pakistan in 1947*

ruler here was a Hindu, but most of his people were Muslims. There were two main political parties in the state; one friendly with the Muslim League, the other led by a Muslim, Sheikh Abdullah, but friendly with Congress.

The Pakistanis naturally thought this state should join Pakistan. When the ruler delayed doing so, they allowed Muslim tribesmen to invade Kashmir. The ruler appealed for troops from India, and said he would join India. The Indian government agreed, but said there should later be a pleciscite – a vote – to decide whether the people of Kashmir wanted to stay with India or join Pakistan.

The tribesman were halted, but the fighting soon became a battle between the regular troops of India and Pakistan. But at the end of 1948 a ceasefire was arranged, leaving the best part of the state in India's hands. Both countries accepted a United Nations resolution calling for a plebiscite.

In the years that followed there were endless talks about how precisely the plebiscite should be carried out, but no agreement.

15. THE COMMUNIST VICTORY IN CHINA

Civil war starts again

The surrender of Japan in 1945 left the Chinese communists and the Kuomintang free to resume their own civil war. At first it was a race to capture the areas now freed from the Japanese, and the weapons they left behind. The Kuomintang troops advanced in many places, but they could not seize

2. Students of the 'cave university' set up by the Chinese communists near Yenan sing patriotic songs. (About 1943)

Manchuria, China's main industrial area, which Russian troops had occupied just before the war ended.

In early 1946 the Americans arranged a ceasefire, but it soon broke down. Again the Kuomintang troops advanced. Chiang Kai-shek had roughly 3 million troops against the communists' 1 million. His troops were better armed. Though the Americans stopped sending weapons for a short time, the Kuomintang was getting American supplies, while the communists got little from Russia. Chiang had an air force; the communists had none.

The Kuomintang collapses

Yet, from the start of the communist counter-attack in mid 1947, the Kuomintang armies were first on the defensive and then rapidly defeated. As the war raged over north and central China, the communist generals time and again outwitted their opponents. A gigantic battle round Hsuchow, in east central China, late in 1948, ended, after months of fighting, in the death or surrender of more than 500,000 Kuomintang troops.

In 1949 the communists swept down into southern and south-western China. By the end of the year, Chiang Kai-shek and what was left of his armies had fled to Formosa, an island 120 miles off the coast. There they remain today, still claiming to be the only lawful government of China.

Why the Kuomintang lost

Why did the Kuomintang lose? Partly because the communist generals were more skilful and more determined (notably Lin Piao, see chapter 27). Partly because the Americans in 1948 refused to make the huge extra effort – in military training, weapons and aircraft – that might, but probably would not, have turned the tide for the Kuomintang.

But the main reason was that the Kuomintang armies, and the people it governed, did not want to fight. Few of them saw anything worth fighting for.

In the countryside the peasants were ground down by landlords and robbed by soldiers, while communist agitators promised that under communism all that would end. In the cities prices went sky high. Corrupt officials grew rich while everyone else grew poorer. Anyone who criticized was silenced by the police. Communism sounded much better.

The communists take power

So, on October 1, 1949, the communists announced the birth of the Chinese People's Republic, headed by Mao Tse-tung. The most populous country in the world was now ruled by communists.

5. *The communist take-over in China (communist-controlled areas shaded)*

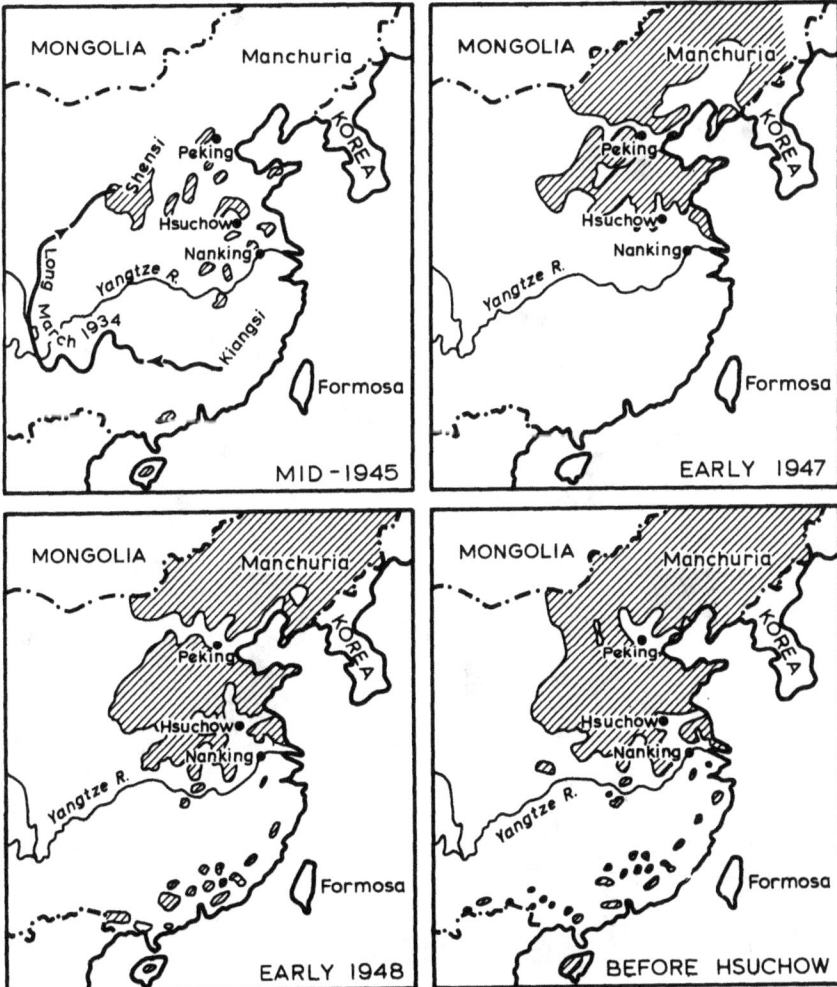

13. *Lin Piao, later the communists' most successful general, and a leading figure in the 'cultural revolution' of 1966, lectures students at the 'cave university' at Yenan*

16. HOW THE COMMUNISTS CHANGED CHINA

The communist aims

The new Chinese government promptly set about changing the Chinese way of life more drastically than at any time in its history. They had two aims: to make China a great, modern, power in the world; and to spread communist ideas, and the power of the Communist Party, so effectively that they could never again be challenged.

Controlling China

First, they set out to extend their control over the whole of China's territory. In the winter of 1949–50 they were preparing to invade Formosa, but were prevented by warnings from the Americans (see chapter 18). In 1950 Chinese troops invaded Tibet, which had once been part of the Chinese Empire but had been independent since 1912. They also had to make sure of other areas, like Tibet, inhabited by people not of Chinese race. These areas account for more than half of China, though for barely one-twentieth of its population. The local people often have links with people across the border (in the Soviet Union and Mongolia, for instance). The Chinese were afraid of outside interference from those countries.

To prevent that, the Chinese have set up local governments that appear to be run by the local people, but that are actually controlled from Peking. Many Chinese have been settled in these areas. But the Chinese did not introduce communist reforms so fast as in other places. Even so, interference with local customs has led to occasional rebellions; in Tibet in 1955–59, and several times in Sinkiang. Yet many of the local people are better off than they ever used to be.

Changing China

But the real problem was to change the Chinese people themselves, and their way of doing things. Most of them were
peasants, who only wanted to have their own land and to be
left to look after it in peace. Some were landlords, others
businessmen. None of their ideas fitted into the communist
way of doing things.

The communists know best

The communists' first principle was that 'the Communist
Party knows best'.

The communists have allowed several non-communist
parties to exist, in accordance with their old 'united front'
idea. These parties mainly include middle-class people. They
do what the Communist Party tell them.

So does the government. Since a new constitution was
adopted in 1954, China has had a State Council (like the
British Cabinet), headed by a Prime Minister, who is helped
by various other ministers. Chou En-lai has been Prime
Minister since 1954, and was Foreign Minister also until 1958
when Chen Yi (another founder-member of the Chinese
Communist Party, see chapter 9) got the job.

There is also a kind of parliament, the National People's
Congress, with about 3,000 elected members. Elections in
China amount to voting for a single list of candidates approved
by the Communist Party, with no other choice. But the
members are not altogether unrepresentative. However the
NPC meets rarely and has never been known to do anything
but approve the policies of the government.

All important decisions are taken by the Communist Party.
Though it grew from 3 million members in 1949 to 17 million
in 1962, it is still only a tiny part of China's 700 million people.
And in fact the decisions are taken by the very small group of
men right at the top, led by the Chairman, Mao Tse-tung.
Many of them, of course, also have government posts. The
same is true right down to the lowest levels of local government; at every level there is a corresponding Communist
Party branch, with members in leading positions of the local
government.

The communists also control all newspapers, books, the

radio and so on. It is not only illegal to spread non-communist ideas, but almost impossible.

They keep firm control too of the armed forces. Mao Tse-tung, believing that 'power grows out of the barrel of a gun', has been determined that 'the party must control the gun, not the gun the party'. There are party committees in every army unit, and much time is spent not on military training but in studying communist ideas.

Spreading the message

But not even a communist government can simply announce that everything must change overnight. The communists have moved rapidly, but they have gone step by step, and each time they make a change they put on a great campaign to persuade the people to accept it.

'Persuasion' in fact has meant a mixture of propaganda and terror. The lead is taken by the Communist Party itself. Once the top men have decided what is to be done, they tell the government and the civil servants. At the same time the party members, all the way down to the local branches, see that it is done and 'educate' the people. After their work, workers go to political discussion meetings led by party members. Newspapers, the radio, posters, loudspeakers, plays and books all carry the message. Even lessons in the schools are made to fit the party line. Huge rallies are held. Meetings are organized by the many 'mass' organizations open to non-communists, such as trade unions, peasants' or students' organizations, to explain the new decision.

The purpose of all this is that everyone should think (and do) the same thing, whether the slogan is 'hate America' or 'kill flies'. Those who disagree are nowadays invited to criticize themselves until they see the light. Anyone unusually stubborn may find himself labelled 'reactionary' or 'counter-revolutionary' and may be sentenced to 'reform' himself through forced labour. In the first few years of communist rule he might well have been put to death.

Are communist methods wrong?

These methods sound very unpleasant, and they are. The best arguments in favour of them are that:

1. The communists are trying to do (and have done) a tremendous amount in a huge country in a very short time. To get things moving is the hardest task in an old-fashioned country, as the Indians have found. *Perhaps* free discussion is a luxury that such countries cannot afford. For them, the choice between democracy and dictatorship is not an easy one.

2. The Chinese communists know they have many enemies outside China. They fear their enemies will use any disagreement inside China to try to overthrow them.

An interruption

The 'cultural revolution' that began in 1966 (see chapter 27) has upset this tidy pattern of orders coming down from the top and being distributed uniformly by every possible means. Now that there *are* open disagreements among the party and government leaders, there are rival 'messages' coming from the top (and sometimes from lower down). But the pattern remains basically true. If and when China's leaders settle their differences, things probably, though not certainly, will go on as they did before.

17. CHANGES IN CHINA: 1949–1957

Advancing in jerks

China's story since 1949 has been one of advance towards a more communist way of doing things, followed often by a pause or a slight retreat – because the communist way did not work, or the people resisted it – and then a further advance. The communists insist that 'politics must be in command' and have sometimes rushed ahead with their way of doing things, based on political theories, when common sense would have told them to go slower, or to do something different. Then the more practical men in the party have objected.

The communists say that everyone must be 'red and expert' meaning both communist-minded and good at his job. But there have been constant arguments, among the party leaders, between those who put more emphasis on being 'red' and the 'experts' who are more concerned in getting things done. This has been true in farming, in industry and in the armed forces.

Communist agriculture

The greatest change has been in the countryside. In 1950, a law was brought in confiscating the land of landlords and giving it to the poorest peasants. This was accompanied by a savage campaign against the landlords. There was a similar campaign at the same time against all 'counter-revolution-aries', i.e. anti-communists. Millions of people were 'tried' before howling mobs and 800,000 were executed. The government encouraged farmers to form 'mutual aid teams' of about twenty families. But the peasants still owned their own land, animals, tools and so on.

From 1953, co-operatives began to be formed. Land and

14. *Science, nationalism and communism go together. This electron microscope was built, says the Chinese news agency, 'entirely of Chinese materials . . . through the concerted efforts of Chinese scientists, technicians and workers'*

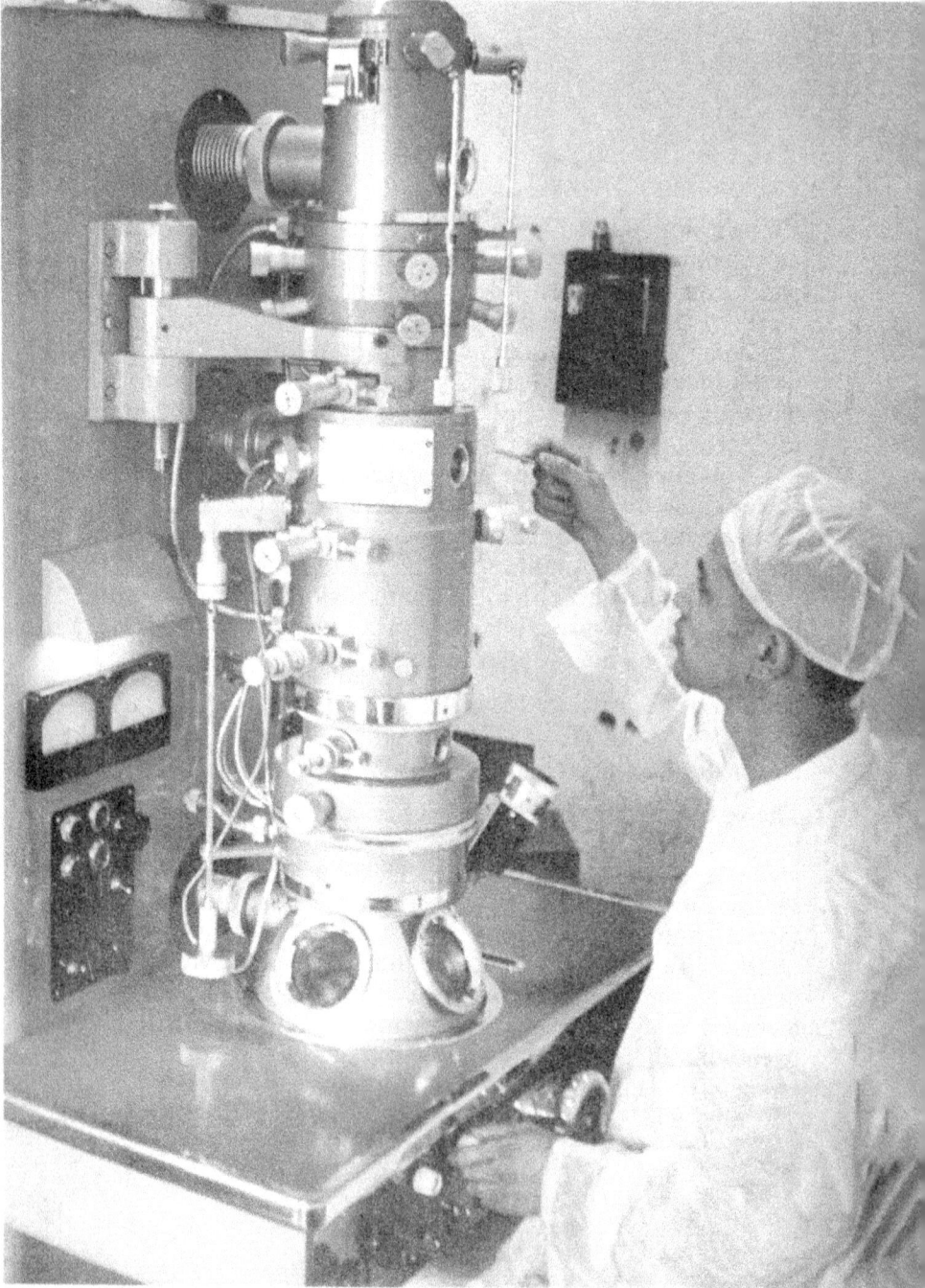

animals were pooled, though the peasant still (in theory) had the right to withdraw from the co-operative. Many peasants opposed this, and there was argument inside the party.

But in 1955 Mao Tse-tung ruled that the forming of co-operatives must be pushed ahead faster than ever. By the end of 1956 virtually all the peasants were organized in this way.

In 1958 came the most revolutionary step of all, when groups of co-operatives were formed into 'people's communes' during the 'great leap forward'. This is fully described in chapter 25.

Communist industry and trade

In industry and trade the problem was simpler. There were not very many factories in China anyway.

From 1949 to 1954 the government seized foreign-owned businesses, and those of Chinese who had fled abroad, for the state. But they allowed private businesses to carry on under heavy restrictions, which got worse as the years went on.

In 1955 the remaining private businesses were transformed into 'joint' state-private enterprises. The former owners now only got a small yearly payment according to the value of the business. This change was almost complete by the end of 1956. Meanwhile small private businessmen had been organized into co-operatives.

Most selling (and all foreign trade) came into the hands of the state.

The 'great leap forward' of 1958 brought further changes.

Developing industry

Meanwhile, enormous efforts were being made to turn China into a modern industrial country. Hundreds of new state-owned factories were set up. In the first five-year plan (1953–57) seven times as much was spent on industry as on farming. Nearly all of that was for heavy industry – iron and steel, mining, chemicals and so on – and very little for making goods such as clothes and shoes for the ordinary people. Their turn was to come later.

At the same time many new schools, universities, hospitals and so on were built. Many parts of the country where these things had been almost unknown now had them, and many poor people who could never have afforded to use them now had the chance.

There is no doubt that communist methods have worked in China. More is produced, in factories and farms, than ever before. Non-communist methods might have done that. But it is unlikely that non-communist methods would have done so much for the common people. Most ordinary Chinese are better off than they were before 1949. They have more to eat, more clothes, better houses, more schools for their children.

Those who used to own land are probably sorry that it is now public property. And everyone has lost the right to disagree, to think for himself. Little of this was allowed by the Kuomintang; the communists allow none whatever.

The 'Hundred Flowers movement'

Most people, in fact, may not want to think for themselves. But the few who do – writers, teachers, and other well-educated people – have suffered under communism. In 1954 a campaign was launched against those who had dared to disagree. But in 1956 there came the 'Hundred Flowers movement'; the communists began to encourage people to say what they thought, with the slogan 'let a hundred flowers bloom, let a hundred schools of thought contend'. The flood of criticism that followed was too much for the Communist Party (even though few people criticized the communist system itself, only the way it worked). In mid 1957 the communists counterattacked; the critics were suppressed and made to confess that they were wrong. Since then the writers have been kept quiet.

18. CHINA AND THE WORLD: 1949–1957

Changing attitudes

Since 1949, the Chinese have not always got on well with other countries. Indeed, since 1957 they have hardly tried to. Their position can be summed up thus:

1. Towards the United States: enmity, right from the start.

2. Towards the Soviet Union and communist countries in Europe: friendship at first, followed by a quarrel which has grown steadily worse since about 1957.

3. Towards the neutral countries such as India, Egypt, and most newly independent countries: suspicion from 1949 to 1951; friendship from 1951 to 1957; a cooling-off, or even enmity, since 1957.

China and the Americans

The Chinese communists had good reason to dislike the United States. It was the most pro-capitalist and anti-communist of all countries. Besides, the Americans had been the chief allies of Chiang Kai-shek.

The two countries soon had several things to quarrel about:

1. The Korean war. In mid 1950, communists from North Korea invaded non-communist South Korea. The United Nations sent troops – most of them American – to help South Korea. They drove the North Koreans far back into their own half of the country. As the war came near the Chinese border, the Chinese warned that they might take part. Suddenly they let loose their army – saying the soldiers were 'volunteers' to help Korea – and the Americans, taken by surprise were driven right down to the south again. But they fairly soon drove the Chinese back to about the middle of Korea, and there the fighting dragged on till a truce was arranged in 1953.

2. Formosa. When Chiang Kai-shek fled there in 1949, the Americans at first seemed ready to let the communists pursue him, and to recognize the communists as the legal government of China. But as soon as the Korean War began, they announced that their fleet would prevent either side attacking the other. They started sending weapons for the Kuomintang army in Formosa. In 1954–55, and again in 1958, when the communists shelled some small islands, just off the mainland coast, that were still held by the Kuomintang, the Americans threatened that this might lead to war with the United States.

The Americans still recognize the Kuomintang government as the government of China. They have always blocked any attempt to take the United Nations seat that belongs to 'China' away from the Kuomintang and give it to the communists.

3. 'Encirclement' and 'subversion'. Since the Korean War began, the Americans have made alliances with several countries round China: South Korea, Japan, the Kuomintang in Formosa, the Philippines, Thailand, Pakistan. In 1954 they organized the South-East Asia Treaty Organization, an alliance of the United States, Britain, France, Australia, New Zealand, Pakistan, Thailand and the Philippines. The Americans said this was to deter communist countries from attacking others. The Chinese say it was to 'encircle' and threaten them. The Americans in turn accuse the Chinese of 'subversion', of trying to overthrow the governments of non-communist countries by organizing rebellions against them.

China and the Soviet Union

In 1950, Mao Tse-tung and Stalin, the Russian leader, signed a treaty of alliance between the two countries. Soon thousands of Russian engineers, Russian machines and money were at work building China's new factories. China's army received Russian weapons.

But Stalin also demanded a price. The Chinese agreed to let the Russians go on using the Port Arthur naval base and to share control of the railways in Manchuria until the end of 1952. It was probably Stalin who forced the Chinese to join in the Korean War.

After Stalin's death, the new Russian leader, N. S. Khrushchev, agreed in 1954 that Russia would lend more money and help build more factories. The Russians had already given up control of the railways, and they agreed to move entirely out of Port Arthur. They also agreed to help the Chinese in nuclear science; for peaceful purposes, they said.

This was the high point of friendship between the two countries.

But in 1956, when Khrushchev denounced Stalin for having been a tyrant, the Chinese were worried. They feared (rightly) that their communist allies in Russia were growing soft. Chapter 25 shows how the quarrel developed.

China and the neutrals

After (and even before) 1949, the Chinese tried to encourage communist rebellions even in countries such as India that were already free from colonial rule. They abused Nehru as a 'lackey of imperialism'.

But from about 1951 they began to talk of 'peaceful coexistence' between communist and non-communist countries, even capitalist ones. In 1954 they helped to settle the war in French Indochina between the French and the Vietnamese nationalists. The 'five principles of coexistence' that later became popular in 'non-aligned' countries first appeared in a treaty between China and India in 1954 (see chapter 24).

China against imperialism

But the Chinese never forgot their dislike of European imperialism. Chou En-lai, China's Prime Minister, played a leading part at a meeting in 1955, at Bandung, in Indonesia, of African and Asian leaders, who issued strong statements of 'Afro-Asian solidarity' against imperialism, The Chinese have often encouraged anti-colonial movements with money, weapons and training in guerrilla warfare.

19. THE KUOMINTANG
IN FORMOSA

Two 'governments of China'

After 1949, Chiang Kai-shek and his supporters settled down in Formosa. Though they only govern about 12 million people, they still claim to be the legal government of China. They promise that one day they will return and reconquer the mainland. They maintain a huge army of 600,000 men, mostly armed and paid for by their allies, the Americans. Occasionally from their offshore islands (see chapter 18) they make commando raids on the communist mainland.

The two rival governments exchange abuse on the radio and in the newspapers. They each try to win the support of other countries throughout the world. The communists promise that one day they will reunite Formosa with the mainland. But the Americans prevent either side from launching an attack. If Formosa and the mainland are ever to be reunited it will probably not be by war but through agreement after Chiang Kai-shek's death.

Formosa under the Kuomintang

Inside Formosa, Chiang Kai-shek's men have governed much better than they ever did in mainland China. There is not much democracy. The mainlanders who came across in 1949 with Chiang Kai-shek (about 2 million out of 12 million) hold most of the real power. Some of the native Formosans resent this.

But Formosa is prosperous. The Americans have provided a great deal of money to build up industries and improve farming – so successfully that since 1965 Formosa has been able to do without this help. Between 1949 and 1955 the government carried out land reforms, first compulsorily reducing rents, then taking land from the landlords and selling it to the tenant-farmers. As in most poor countries, this reform was actually much more useful to the people than the right to a free vote.

By Asian standards, Formosa today is a reasonably well-run country, and its people are reasonably free.

5. *1965. American anti-aircraft missiles supplied to Chiang Kai-shek's forces in Formosa. The parade is just passing his presidential palace*

20.   POLITICS IN FREE INDIA

Problems of freedom

When India and Pakistan became free in 1947, both countries had three main problems.

1. How the country was to be kept united, and how it was to be governed.

2. How to give a better life to its millions of poor people.

3. How it was to behave towards its neighbours and the other countries of the world.

This and the next four chapters deal with these problems in turn.

Uniting India

Ever since British India was torn in two in 1947, most Indians have been determined that their country should not be divided again.

The first job of the new Indian government, headed by Nehru, was to make sure that India was indeed united as a single country. They had to persuade the 560 princes to make their states part of it (see chapter 14).

This job was given to Vallabhbhai Patel, the most important Congress leader after Nehru and Gandhi and the toughest of the three. He soon got most of the princes to agree. But the Muslim ruler of Hyderabad – the largest state of all, stretching across central India – tried to remain independent. In 1948, the Indian army invaded his state and made it part of India, as, probably, most of the people wanted.

The invasion of Goa

There were also tiny areas owned by France and Portugal. The French, rather slowly, agreed to quit. The Portuguese simply refused. After years of trying to persuade them, Nehru lost patience. In 1961, the Indians invaded Goa and two other small Portuguese territories. Many foreigners were shocked, particularly because Indians had so often talked about 'non-violence'. But to Indians this was simply the completion of India's freedom. Not all the Goans were happy, though.

Kashmir and Nagaland

The Indians have also had to prevent their country being torn apart. They have had trouble in Kashmir (see chapter 14), and from the Naga tribesmen who live in the mountains and jungles of India's eastern border. The Nagas are mostly Christians and quite different in their habits from the Indians in the plains. Many do not want to be part of India. In 1956 a rebellion began in Nagaland, which the Indian army tried to suppress very severely, until there was a ceasefire in 1964.

The Indians are not just being selfish in Kashmir or Nagaland. They really fear that if they let some people split away from India many others may try.

Governing India

Then, how was India to be governed? The new rulers had been brought up with British ideas, and in many ways they copied Britain, while making allowances for India's great size.

A new constitution was brought into force in 1950. It made India a republic, headed by a president (where Britain has a king or queen). But the real power belongs to the Prime Minister and his Cabinet, as in Britain. There is a parliament, made up of a 'House of the People' (like the House of Commons) with elected members, and a 'Council of States', whose members are chosen by the different state assemblies. The country is divided into seventeen states, each with its chief minister and cabinet, and legislative assembly.

The state governments are far more powerful than any local council in Britain. The central government cannot just give them orders, it must persuade them and get their co-operation.

Trouble about language

Nearly every state has a separate language of its own. There are fourteen important languages in India, and the only one spoken everywhere (but only by educated people) is English. Indians sometimes fear that their country will split up and the states will become separate countries.

For this very reason, the state boundaries at first did not correspond to 'language-boundaries'. But in 1952 riots by people who spoke one particular language forced the central government to give them a state of their own. In 1956 the whole map was redrawn, giving each important language-group a state of its own; it seemed safer to give way to feelings about language than to resist them. In two areas the rule was not followed. In both rioting eventually forced the government to change its mind.

English or Hindi?

There has also been trouble about the official language, the language used in government business. The constitution said this should be English until 1965, and then Hindi, a north Indian language. Less than half India's people speak Hindi, but it is not hard for north Indians to learn. But it is quite unlike south Indian languages.

Though Nehru had said that English would be used after 1965 as well as Hindi, southerners thought they would be at a disadvantage. As the day for the change approached, there were riots in southern India.

The change has made little real difference. English is still commonly used. But the argument continues. Many norther-ners say it is absurd that India's official language should be a foreign one which few Indians speak. Southerners say that at least English is spoken everywhere, unlike Hindi, so no area has an unfair advantage.

Meanwhile, in the different states the use of the local state language is becoming more and more common.

Religion can cause trouble

Religion also sometimes causes trouble. Though all religions should be treated alike, the existence of Pakistan makes difficulties for India's 50 million Muslims. Sometimes they feel they are not trusted by the Hindu majority. Though they are given a fair chance of getting government jobs, they find it hard to get jobs in business, which is mostly controlled by Hindus.

Very occasionally, there is violence between Hindus and Muslims, and there are some unscrupulous politicians who secretly whip up trouble to win support from one group or the other. One of the four important opposition parties is openly a Hindu party. Nehru himself believed firmly in 'secularism', in treating all religions equally. But some Congress politicians only pay lip-service to it. Politicians are seldom much better than the people who elect them, and the typical Indian still has strong feelings in favour of his own religious group. Hindu political feeling is a growing force.

No Sikhistan

The Sikhs (see chapter 2) are a different problem. Before 1947, some Sikhs wanted the country to be divided not just into two but into three, so they would have 'Sikhistan', a country of their own between India and West Pakistan. This idea was revived later in the demand for a 'Punjabi-speaking' state (most Punjabi-speakers being Sikhs).

The government, knowing this was really a demand for a Sikh state, and fearing what it might lead to, resisted it till 1966. Then, for fear of Sikh rioting, the existing Punjab state was divided in two – but in such a way that there are only just more Sikhs than Hindus even in the new 'Punjabi-speaking' state.

Congress and the opposition parties

A country so divided by language and religion, and with so many problems, might well have chosen dictatorship by one party as its way of government. But the Congress leaders chose democracy, roughly on the British pattern, and have stuck to it. There are many political parties, and free elections.

Because of its work for freedom, Congress has always been the most popular party. In the first three elections (1952, 1957, 1962) it always won about three-quarters of the seats in parliament, though it did worse in 1967. The central government has always been formed by Congress. So, with very rare exceptions, until 1967, were the state governments.

This was valuable for India. It made it easier to settle disagreements between state and central governments. It also meant that most of the real political argument was between different sections of Congress, not between Congress and the opposition parties. Though Nehru in his seventeen years as Prime Minister (1947 to 1964) could nearly always get his way inside Congress, these arguments went on. Since his death they have come more into the open.

There are four main opposition parties. The *Swatantra* ('freedom') Party is against socialism. It is supported mainly by businessmen and, in some areas, by the princes and their former subjects. The *Jan Sangh* ('people's party') appeals to Hindu feeling and is violently hostile to Pakistan. The Communist Party began in 1948 by trying to raise a rebellion in one part of India, but then adopted democratic ways. In 1957 communists were able to form a state government in Kerala, a south Indian state, but this was dismissed after rioting organized by Congress. Later the communists split into two parties: the 'right-wing' communists, who believe in seeking power through parliament, and the 'left' communists, who believe in revolution.

The 1967 elections brought great changes. The Congress Party's majority in the central parliament was cut sharply. In most state assemblies it remained the largest single party. But in no less than eight states, covering over half of India's population, opposition parties, by forming 'united fronts', were able to take power.

This meant that for the first time the Congress central government had to learn to get along with non-Congress state governments. In two of them, communists were the largest element.

It also meant that the new state governments, being formed from parties that were only united in disliking Congress, were always in danger of breaking up.

21. POLITICS IN PAKISTAN

Pakistan's troubles

Pakistan has had a far harder time than India. Its first difficulty was in surviving at all. When the Hindus fled in 1947, Pakistan lost most of its businessmen and administrators. It had to start from scratch. To make things worse, there were huge numbers of Muslim refugees from India to be looked after.

Two more misfortunes came in quick succession. Jinnah died in late 1948, and in 1951 the Prime Minister, Liaqat Ali Khan, the only other man respected throughout Pakistan, was murdered. From then on, there was endless political trouble and uncertainty.

The great difficulty was in deciding how Pakistan should be governed. It took nine years to draw up a constitution. The main disagreements were:

1. How important should Muslim religious ideas be in the way the country was governed? Many modern-minded politicians said 'not much'. But the religious teachers, who have great influence, disagreed.

2. What was to be the relationship between the east wing and the west wing of the country? The two are very different. The east is much poorer, and is suspicious of being dominated by the west. Their people speak different languages. When it was suggested in 1952 that Urdu, the language of the west, should be the national language, there were riots in the east. The Muslim League was still powerful in the west; in the east leading politicians turned against it, and it was routed in local elections there in 1954.

3. Should West Pakistan, made up of several different states, continue to have several different governments or only one? In 1955 it was turned into one unit.

4. What power should the central government have over the provincial governments?

Corruption, intrigue and incompetence

These disagreements were made far worse by the intrigues, corruption and weakness of the politicians. There was no strong man, and no strong party like Congress in India. While they worked out their own constitution, the Pakistanis had kept the system of government inherited from the British, with a Governor-General as head of the country, and a Prime Minister to run it. After 1951, the Governor-General started to interfere in the government. He dismissed the Prime Minister in 1953 and the whole central assembly in 1954.

Things became no better after the new constitution was brought in, in 1956. There was disorder and political intrigue. The politicians were busier making money for themselves by various dishonest means than in helping to run the country. So were many of the civil servants.

In late 1958, the army kicked the civilian politicians out and took power.

Ayub Khan's new system

The Commander-in-Chief, General Ayub Khan (born 1907) soon became President. The new régime was popular and started well. Corruption and tax-evasion were stopped. Prices were brought down. The slums full of refugees round Karachi, the capital, were cleared away and the refugees properly rehoused.

President Ayub had decided that the British type of democracy just did not work in a country where most people could not read, and where the politicians were so. self-interested. The army had banned all political parties. Later Ayub allowed them, and became leader of one part of the Muslim League. But the constitution he brought in, in 1962, was very different from the old one.

It gives the President great powers. There is a national assembly and provincial assemblies for East and West Pakistan. But they have comparatively little power. The biggest change was in the method of election. Before, tens of thousands of people voted to elect a single member of the assembly. Most of them could know nothing about the rival candidates. Now, there would be 80,000 'basic democrats', each elected by only 1,000 or 1,500 people. The 'basic democrats' in turn would elect members of the national or provincial assemblies. So, at each level, the rival candidates would be quite well known to the electors.

The 'basic democrats' in each area also help in local government. This system seems to have worked well in helping get things done – building roads, digging water-channels and so on – in the countryside; and in giving the local people a fair chance of deciding what is to be done.

Basic democracy or parliamentary democracy?

The 80,000 'basic democrats' also elect the President. The first real presidential election was held in early 1965. Ayub was opposed by Jinnah's sister, who was backed by most of the opposition parties. The election, first of the new 'basic democrats', then by them of the president, became a trial of strength between the new system and the old.

Miss Jinnah said Pakistan should go back to the old, British type of democracy. She won much support in East Pakistan. But Ayub won the election easily – to no-one's great surprise: one of the accusations Ayub's opponents made against him was that he had designed his 'basic democracy' so that the comparatively small number of electors would be easy for the government to bribe or influence.

East against West

Miss Jinnah's East Pakistani supporters were not simply voting for her idea of democracy. Many were mainly voting against the central government and against West Pakistanis. President Ayub Khan's biggest problem now is to unite the Pakistanis of east and west. People in the east are resentful because they are poorer, and most of the new factories are built in the west. Even in the east most industries are controlled by West Pakistanis. Ayub Khan's government has done something to level things up, but not nearly enough.

Asia's problems are different

It is too soon to tell whether the Indian system or the Pakistani one works better, or how long either will last. India's looks more democratic (and certainly the Indian government allows more comment and criticism in the newspapers). But it may not necessarily be better for the people.

As these two chapters have shown, the new countries that the British left behind have different problems (and more of them) than old, well-established countries. The methods of government that seem natural in one country may, or may not, seem natural – or be successful – somewhere else.

22. ESCAPE FROM POVERTY

Poor farms, few factories

We have seen in chapters 16 and 17 how the communist Chinese built up China's economy: by state organization, public ownership, and, when necessary, compulsion. What about India and Pakistan?

They too had great problems. Most of their farms were inefficient. They had few factories. In 1947 undivided India could produce all the cotton goods it needed; nearly enough steel, but only because little was used; paper and cement for half its needs. Light engineering was growing. But most kinds of machinery and chemicals had to be imported. The British rulers had not ignored these needs, but basically they felt the government's job was to govern and let businessmen get on by themselves.

How can poor countries advance?

Especially in India, the new rulers were not satisfied. It was intolerable to them that their people should live in poverty while Westerners were rich. But they did not believe in compulsion, as the Chinese communists did. They were not prepared to bring everything, farms and factories alike, into public ownership.

This was the great question: could poor countries modernize their farms and factories without either the suffering caused by unrestricted 'free enterprise' (as happened in England and America) or the suffering caused by unrestricted state control (as in Russia and China)?

India chose a middle way. Nehru was a socialist. He believed private businessmen might exist but should be controlled. He believed in public ownership of industry. He believed in planning, having admired Russia's five-year plans. He also thought the government would have to do part of the job: India's businessmen just would not have the money, or be prepared to risk it, for some of the huge factories that were needed.

This, broadly, is what India has done, though Nehru had to compromise. Many Congress members were not socialists. They have been strong enough to ensure that, though Congress says it aims towards a 'socialist society', those who have done best out of the growth of Indian industry have been the businessmen, not the common people.

Gandhi against industry

Others, notably Gandhi himself, did not want huge industries at all. They thought every man should produce what he could for himself; for instance, by spinning and weaving his own cloth, as Gandhi did. If factories were needed, there should be many small ones, not one big one. That would give jobs and

16. *Indian farming today. Traditional bullock-cart, modern warehouse – and modern methods: the warehouse belongs to a farmers' co-operative society which distributes fertilizer and improved seeds to its members*

money to millions of people living in the countryside – as four out of five Indians still do. Besides, they said, it is better for a man to work in his own village than move to the crowded slums typical of many Indian cities.

Some attention is still given to these ideas. 'Cottage' industries are important producers, for instance, of cloth, soap and matches. The growth of unemployment in India has recently made some people more favourable to the Gandhians. But, on the whole, they lost the argument.

Setting up industry

So in 1950 India set out on its first five-year plan. The government has taken the lead. For instance, three great new steel-mills have been built, all publicly owned. Railway engines, lathes, aeroplanes, fertilizers, medicines are produced in government factories. At the same time ordinary firms have set up hundreds of new factories.

Changing the farms

Farming too is being improved. Since rain only falls for a few months in the year, several vast dams have been built (the British did this too) to store water and provide hydro-electric power. New kinds of seeds are being introduced, to give larger crops. Instead of their age-old methods, farmers are learning new ones from government-trained experts. Chemical fertilizers, for instance, were little used fifteen years ago, but are now eagerly bought.

Just as important, the whole way of life in India's half-million villages is slowly being changed. Land-reform laws have taken land from the landlords and given it to their tenants or to landless labourers. Co-operative banks are replacing village money-lenders who used to charge interest at twenty-five or fifty per cent a year. Co-operative marketing societies let the peasant get a fair share of the profits of his crops, instead of the grain-merchant taking most. New roads, schools, medical services and electric power supplies give the Indian villager chances that his parents never had.

The results

None of this is happening fast. There is much confusion, and many things go wrong. But it is happening, as some figures show:

	1950	1965
Population (millions)	361	495
Grain crops (million tons)	55	80
Fertilizer used (thousand tons)	60	850
Villages with electricity	3,000	43,000
Cloth woven (million yards)	4,700	8,000
Steel (thousand tons)	1,050	6,000
Children at school (millions)	23	68

Not good enough

These figures are impressive. And yet most of them are well below the targets aimed at. India has not done as well as some other poor countries. And it is still far behind: Britain, for instance, with one-tenth as many people, produces four times as much steel.

Why did India not do as well as it hoped? And what is being done to put things right?

1. The population has grown too fast. Better medical services mean that more children live to grow up, fewer people die of disease. The children have to be fed and clothed till they can look after themselves. More food and goods are available – but they have to be shared among more people. So a campaign for birth-control has been started.

2. Farming methods have not improved enough. A Japanese farmer can grow two or three times as much rice on an acre of land as an Indian one. This is partly because peasants just do not change their habits overnight; partly because not enough was done to teach them; partly because, when they had learned, the improved seeds or fertilizers, for instance, were not available. Too much attention was paid, in 1955–62, to industry. Now the balance has been changed towards agriculture.

3. Mistakes were made in industry. The government was determined to control Indian businessmen and, still more, foreign ones. But its own industries – the steel-mills, for instance – were often badly managed. It would not let foreign companies put up new fertilizer factories, but did not build enough itself. Controls sometimes caused long delays for private firms. Private firms also made mistakes. In some

industries too many new factories were built: they could not get enough raw materials, or sell all their products, and had to work at half-speed. Slowly these problems are being sorted out.

Difficulties, but not failure

There are many difficulties still. Politicians talk much, but often do little. Civil servants often take far too long to deal with important business. The universities have grown so fast that the students are over-crowded, under-educated and dis-contented. And there are too few jobs for all the new graduates. But on the whole India's middle way has worked.

Pakistan's choice

Pakistan has taken a different way forward. Its problems in 1947 were even greater than India's. There was enough food, but very few factories indeed. The mills which had used the

17. *It may not look like it, but this is a revolution. These girls are Pakistani medical students. Education for women used to be almost unknown among Muslims*

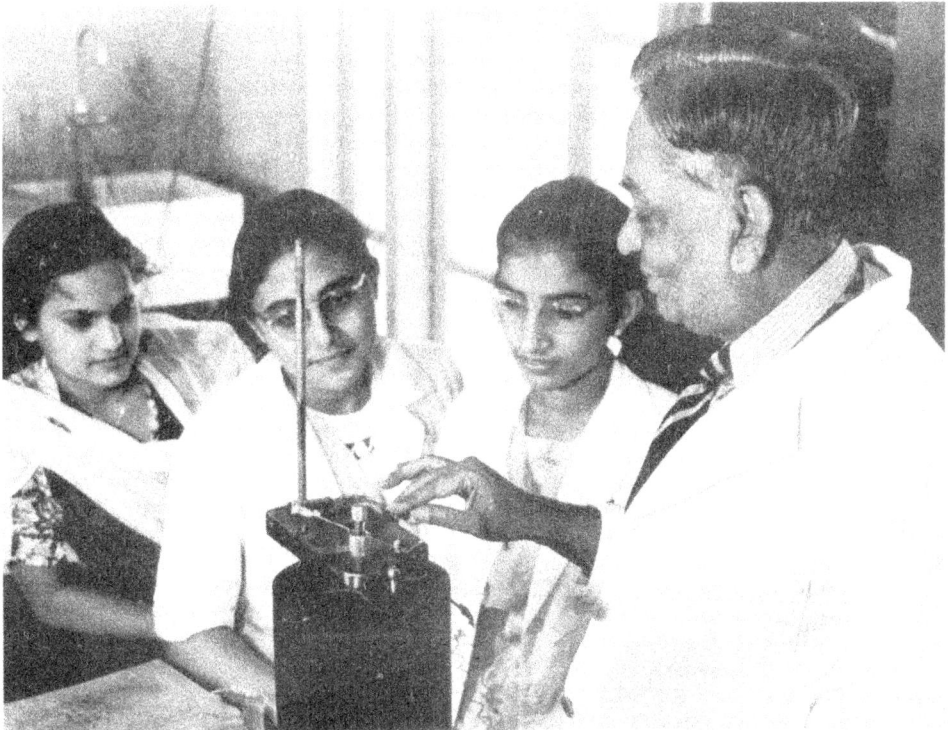

cotton grown in West Pakistan, or the jute grown in East Pakistan, were now in a foreign country. East Pakistan was especially hard hit. Its industrial centre, and only good port, was Calcutta – now in India.

The Muslim leaders had thought much less than the Congress ones about economic matters. They saw that the government would have to help get industries going, but they did not seek to control them. So foreign firms have put in money, and private businessmen have been able to make fortunes without much restriction. This has mostly happened in West Pakistan. The government has helped sometimes by starting industries and then selling them to private firms.

In the countryside, less has been done than in India for the ordinary people. The landlords used to be powerful in West Pakistan, and for years blocked any land reforms. But Ayub Khan brought in reforms in 1959, though they were still fairly generous to the landlords. In East Pakistan, however, there have been fairly strict laws since 1950. Ayub Khan also introduced a 'rural works programme'; the government provides money, and the villagers labour, to build things such as roads that they need.

Who benefits?

In the 1950s India's method seemed to be working best, in the early 1960s Pakistan's. But in both countries the gap between rich and poor has remained as wide as ever. As an example: in Britain the managing director of a firm may earn six times as much as a factory worker, but in India the director earns thirty times as much. Yet an Indian factory worker is rich compared to many Indian peasants. There are the same differences in Pakistan. In both countries it is possible that the people may turn violently against the government because of this.

23. FOREIGN AID

Foreign aid helps in two ways

Both India and Pakistan have been much helped by 'foreign aid' – gifts, or loans, from foreign countries. This helps in two ways: (a) the government has more money to spend on factories or dams; (b) the country has more pounds or dollars, for instance, to buy goods from countries that will not take payment in rupees. This is useful because since the early 1950s neither India nor Pakistan has been able to sell to foreigners as much as it wants to buy from them.

The Americans give most

Both India and Pakistan get most foreign aid from the Americans. Other important amounts come from West Germany, Japan, Britain and France. Russia and east European communist countries have given a fair amount to India, a little to Pakistan. China has given Pakistan some since the two countries became friendly after 1961. India's three new steel-works were all put up with foreign aid; from Britain, West Germany and Russia. The Russians are to build a fourth one.

An important kind of foreign aid has been American wheat. The American government buys surplus wheat from its own farmers and sends it for the Indian or Pakistani governments to sell in their own countries. That not only makes them richer. It is essential if their people are not to starve if there is a bad harvest. Because of a drought, in 1966, for instance America had to send India 8 million tons and Pakistan about 2 million.

Aid has disadvantages too

But foreign aid has disadvantages. The loans have to be repaid one day (and by now there are few outright gifts). The aid-giving governments usually insist their aid must be spent on goods from their countries, which may not be the best or cheapest available.

Aid has political effects. The Americans, especially, tend to think that countries which get so much from them should be on their side in international disputes. In 1965 they delayed their offer of aid to Pakistan, to prevent it becoming too friendly with China.

Particularly since 1963, they have also insisted that countries which they help must be doing their best to help themselves – which means what Americans think is best. In 1965 they cut off aid to India and Pakistan when the two countries went to war. Why should they help countries that were wasting their money on war, the Americans asked. In 1966 they forced the Indian government to give up some of its controls on foreign and Indian firms, and to devalue the rupee. The Americans may possibly have been right in both cases. But naturally Indians and Pakistanis disliked being told what they must and must not do.

Many countries use aid

Other countries give and get aid. China used to get it from Russia (see chapters 18 and 25), and gives it to countries in Asia and Africa that the Chinese hope to win over. India and Pakistan give small amounts.

24. INDIA, PAKISTAN AND THE WORLD

Different approaches

India and Pakistan have not taken the same line towards other countries. India's principle has been to keep out of the quarrel between communist and non-communist countries, to remain 'non-aligned'. Pakistan has done whatever might help it in its own quarrel with India.

India and Pakistan quarrel

The two countries have quarrelled about many things.

1. *Kashmir*. The Pakistanis were infuriated when India blocked all attempts to have a plebiscite held in Kashmir, to decide which country it should belong to (see chapter 14). In 1953 Pakistan agreed to take military aid from the Americans, supposedly for defence against Russia and China, but in fact for strength against India.

Nehru was angry, and soon India's attitude to Kashmir changed. The Indians said (and still say) that circumstances had now changed; they could not be bound by their promise about a plebiscite made years before. The United Nations have tried to solve this quarrel, and the two countries have held talks, but without result.

2. *Minorities*. Each country accuses the other of mistreating its Hindu or Muslim minority. In 1950 refugees began to flood both ways across the East Pakistan–Indian border. Nehru and Liaqat Ali Khan met and agreed that each country should treat its minority just as well as the majority. But since the early 1960s India's expulsion from eastern India of 'illegal Pakistani immigrants' has angered the Pakistanis, who maintain that the people expelled are really Indian Muslims.

3. *Trade*. In 1949, Pakistan refused to devalue its rupee

when India did so, which meant that India would have to pay much more for Pakistani jute and cotton. India cut off all trade for sixteen months.

4. *The Indus waters.* The six rivers in Punjab, which irrigate huge areas of farmland in India and Pakistan, all flow first through India. The Pakistanis feared they would not get a fair share of the water. After years of argument it was agreed in 1960, under American persuasion, that Pakistan should have all the water from the three western rivers, India all the water of the eastern ones. The necessary canals to carry this out are being built with large loans from foreign countries.

America's ally

Pakistan joined two American-inspired alliances: the South-East Asia Treaty Organization in 1954, and the Central Treaty Organization (Pakistan, Iran, Turkey and Britain, plus money from the Americans) in 1955. Until about 1961 it remained hostile to Russia and China and seemed to be America's faithful ally.

Non-aligned India

India, thanks to Nehru, kept firmly out of all military alliances. Though Nehru was a democrat, he said the 'cold war' between communist and non-communist countries was not India's concern. India often helped to calm the quarrel down, for instance in the Korean War. India was the leader in arranging a conference of non-aligned countries in Yugoslavia in 1961.

But the Indians were not neutral on questions of colonialism or racial prejudice, and often spoke against them at the United Nations. Nehru took part in the Afro-Asian conference at Bandung in 1955.

India and Russia

India was naturally on good terms with Russia. The Russians after 1955 took India's side in the Kashmir dispute. They gave India aid for development and later for its army and air force.

India and China

Nehru was keen to be on good terms with China too. He disliked the Chinese occupation of Tibet in 1950, but did not

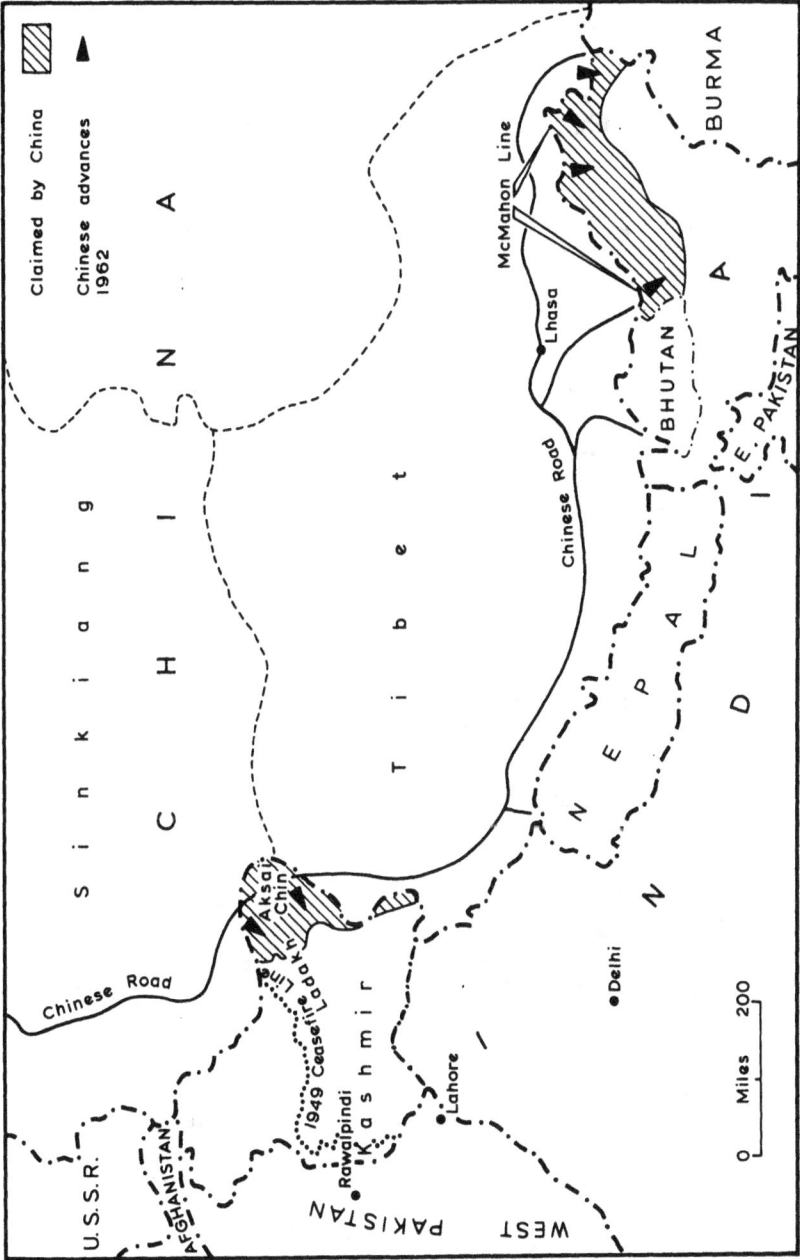

6. *Chinese-Indian-Pakistani rivalries*

protest against it. In 1954 the two countries signed a treaty about Tibet. Chou En-lai visited India in 1956 and was greeted with tremendous enthusiasm and cries of 'Chinese and Indians are brothers'.

But trouble was on the way. China did not agree that India's borders lay where the Indians claimed. In the east they did not recognize the McMahon Line (see chapter 9). In the west, they claimed a large part of Ladakh, the north-eastern corner of Kashmir; in 1955–56 they actually built a road across this corner.

In 1955 and 1956 India protested against Chinese 'intrusions' and against Chinese maps showing the Chinese version of the border. At first, the Chinese said these were simply copies of old maps. But as India's protests multiplied, they changed their tune and in 1959 said that the whole border question was still to be solved. Late that year ten Indian border police were shot in a clash with Chinese troops. Officials of the two countries met in 1960 to discuss the border, but came to no agreement. India would not give up any of its claims (which, on the whole, are better-founded than the Chinese ones). The Chinese probably did not want to settle the quarrel anyway. At that time they were angry that the Indians had welcomed the Dalai Lama, the chief Buddhist of Tibet. He had fled to India in early 1959, after the Chinese had brutally put down a rebellion in Tibet.

In 1962, the quarrel was to become a war (see chapter 25).

Links with Britain

Both India and Pakistan after 1947 were on good terms with Britain, and have generally remained so. This is often taken for granted, yet it might easily never have happened. It is a tribute to the restraint and common sense that both sides showed in the 'struggle' for freedom before 1947, however loudly they denounced each other.

Quite a large part of Indian and Pakistani exports and imports still go to, or come from, Britain. But the proportion is shrinking. So too (though this is less noticed) are the old ties of friendship and respect dating from before 1947.

Members of the Commonwealth

Both India and Pakistan have remained inside the Commonwealth. Indeed, it is thanks to Nehru and his friend V. K. Krishna Menon that the new multi-racial Commonwealth exists. They found a way round the old rule that the King of Britain was automatically head of every Commonwealth country. When India became a republic, Nehru said, it would still recognize the British King as 'head of the Commonwealth' though not as head of India. Many ex-colonies have done the same.

25. CHINA AGAINST ITS NEIGHBOURS

China changes Asia

The whole international scene in Asia has been changed since 1958 by the actions of the Chinese. Inside China the communist leaders have tried to organize everything on more and more communist lines; outside China they have become more and more hostile to anyone who disagrees with them.

The great leap forward

In 1958 the Chinese began what they called 'the great leap forward'. This was supposed to be a leap both towards a completely communist way of living and towards a huge output of farm crops and industrial goods. This was to be done by the organized use of China's own resources, particularly of manpower; being short of money and machines, the Chinese often claim that with the right (communist) ideas man can do everything.

Suddenly in 1958, the co-operative farms were reorganized into 'people's communes', each covering about 20,000 people. Everything became common property, even the peasants' small remaining private gardens. The peasants were organized into production teams almost as if they were in the army. Communal eating-halls and dormitories were built.

Each commune was meant to produce what it needed for itself, even its own machines. There was a campaign to build 'backyard' steel-furnaces. In the towns too communes were set up. Everywhere production targets were set far higher than before.

The great leap fails

The result was a mess. From 1959 to 1961, the harvests were bad. The backyard industries proved to be a waste of energy and materials. In 1959 the government had to admit that fantastic claims of increased production that it had put out a few months earlier were false. Step by step the communes were broken down into smaller units. In 1961 the peasants were given back their gardens and allowed to sell what they grew in them. Again the communists had gone too far too fast.

China and Russia quarrel

Meanwhile, the quarrel with Russia had got steadily worse. The Russians virtually stopped giving China new foreign aid in 1958. In 1959 they refused to provide help in building nuclear weapons, which Khrushchev had promised in 1957. In 1960 suddenly they withdrew from China all the Russian experts, who even took back vital blueprints for new factories with them. That was a fearful blow for China. Meanwhile, the Chinese still had to repay debts for military aid during the Korean War and for Russian equipment left behind in Port Arthur, on top of Russian loans for developing industry.

The reason for the dispute was basically disagreement about the dangers of war, and about the United States. The Russians were scared of nuclear war. They argued that inevitably communism would triumph one day, and meanwhile communists and capitalists must coexist. The Chinese said communism would only triumph through struggle, and that it was the duty of communist countries to encourage 'wars of liberation' in colonial territories and even in independent non-communist countries. They did not care that the result might be war with the United States; the Americans, they said, were 'paper tigers'.

Though both countries tried to paper over their quarrel, it became ever more bitter and more obvious.

War between India and China

One result of China's tough line was war with India. The Chinese since 1959 had been pushing troops forward in Ladakh in the areas they claimed. In early 1962 the Indians began pushing their troops forward. There were several clashes. In October Nehru announced that the Indian army would drive the Chinese out. A week later the Chinese launched a large-scale attack in Ladakh and across the McMahon Line (see map 6, page 105).

It was a complete success. On both fronts the Indians were beaten back. Nehru appealed to Britain and America for weapons, and even (though this was kept secret) for direct help from American bombers. Suddenly in November the Chinese announced a ceasefire and withdrew.

Results of the war

The war had several results:

1. It destroyed Nehru's policy of friendship with China and almost destroyed his policy of non-alignment. Indians saw that the help they needed had come from Britain and America, not from Russia. It was also a blow to the Congress left wing. Their leader, V. K. Krishna Menon, a good friend of the Russians, had been India's Defence Minister, and was blamed for the defeat. Nehru was forced, most unwillingly, to accept his resignation.

2. It greatly offended the Russians, who were angry to see a friendly neutral country attacked, particularly since that might have led to a world war in which Russia would be unwillingly involved.

18. *1960. Nehru welcomes China's Prime Minister Chou En-lai at New Delhi Airport. The garland round Chou's neck is a typical Indian gift for honoured guests*

3. It turned Pakistan away from America and Britain, and towards China.

Pakistan turns towards China

As the price of giving military aid, Britain and the United States forced the Indians to agree to talks with Pakistan about Kashmir. But these talks failed. The Pakistanis then saw their allies arming a country which they regarded as an enemy. Russia was also doing so. The Pakistanis began to look to China as a counter-weight. They had indeed become more friendly with China already: in the middle of the talks on Kashmir, they tactlessly signed an agreement with China settling the border between China and the Pakistan-held part of Kashmir.

Since 1963, the Pakistanis, while remaining members of their American-sponsored alliances have, in fact, become virtually 'non-aligned'. The Americans have been angry; the Pakistanis, reasonably enough, ask why they should remain loyal to allies who are not loyal to them, and hostile to China which does them no harm.

19. *1962. Indian troops on patrol near the Chinese frontier. The 1962 war was fought in conditions like this*

26. INDIA AND PAKISTAN GO TO WAR

The Kashmir quarrel again

The Kashmir quarrel led, in 1965, to another war. It happened like this.

After Kashmir joined India in 1947, its people gradually became discontented. One who did was Sheikh Abdullah, who had become Prime Minister. In 1953 he was suddenly deposed and replaced by a man more loyal to India. Abdullah, who had become a popular hero, was kept in prison till 1958, briefly released, and then imprisoned again.

In early 1964 there were riots in Kashmir against the pro-Indian government. Some rioters were killed by Indian troops. Rumours of a 'slaughter of Muslims' led to anti-Hindu riots in East Pakistan, followed by anti-Muslim riots in eastern India. Hundreds of people were killed, and thousands of refugees began to flow across the border.

India and Pakistan suddenly realized they might be heading for a tragedy like that of 1947. Sheikh Abdullah was released, and allowed to visit Pakistan. It was agreed that Nehru and Ayub Khan should meet.

At that moment, Nehru died. But the new Prime Minister, Lal Bahadur Shastri (1904–1966), was one of the most reasonable Congress leaders. It still seemed possible that the quarrel might be patched up.

But India at that moment was still arranging to get more military aid against China, from Britain, America and Russia. The government also decided that some parts of the Indian constitution that had not previously applied to Kashmir should now do so.

The Pakistanis feared that India was trying to end the dispute by incorporating the Indian part of Kashmir completely in India; and that the Indian army would soon be so strong that there would be nothing Pakistan could do about it.

India and Pakistan at war

The first fighting came in early 1965 over the Rann of Kutch, on the borders of India and West Pakistan. It is completely barren, but a part of it is claimed by both countries. The two armies clashed, but a ceasefire was arranged, and it was agreed to settle the dispute through talks. The danger seemed over.

But within a few weeks there was fighting in Kashmir. Guerrilla fighters crossed the old ceasefire line from Pakistan-held Kashmir into the Indian part of the state. The Indian army took action, and itself crossed the ceasefire line. Then Pakistan's army launched a fierce attack. India retaliated with an attack into West Pakistan itself. For three weeks there was fierce fighting. China threatened to join in, but was warned off by the Americans. America and Russia together persuaded the warring countries to stop.

20. *Indian frontier police on camel-patrol near the West Pakistan border*

An uneasy peace

In early 1966, at a conference arranged by the Russians at Tashkent, Ayub Khan and Shastri agreed on peace terms, under pressure from the Russians and from the Americans (who had cut off aid when the war began and said it would not start again while there was any risk of war).

Shastri died a few hours after signing the agreement. That helped to silence criticism of it in India. Ayub Khan silenced his own critics. But soon the two countries were quarrelling again. Pakistan wanted talks about Kashmir. The Indian government, now headed by Mrs Indira Gandhi (Nehru's daughter), replied as firmly as ever that Kashmir was Indian and would remain Indian. Both countries were soon vigorously rearming, India with weapons from Russia, Pakistan with weapons from China and from Iran.

India and Pakistan after the war

The war caused little damage, but harmed both countries indirectly. American aid was only resumed in 1966, and some factories had to work short time, or shut down, for lack of raw materials from abroad. India suffered particularly. For four years prices had been rising rapidly there, thanks to several bad harvests and to large government spending on armaments since the Chinese War in 1962. Throughout 1966 there was discontent and sometimes rioting in Indian cities over food prices or scarcity. In the months before the 1967 elections there was so much disorder that people began to wonder whether the democratic way of government would survive.

But the real tragedy occurred in the countryside. The failure of the rains in a large part of northern India meant that many people in 1966 and 1967 died of starvation.

27. ON WITH THE REVOLUTION

China after the great leap

China meanwhile was recovering from the failure of the 'great leap'. The 1962 harvest was a good one, and there has been progress since then. No reliable figures exist, but estimates show how China has advanced under communist rule:

	1953	1965
Population (millions)	600	700–750
Grain crops (million tons)	157	190
Coal (million tons)	70	240
Steel (thousand tons)	1,770	11,000

As things got better, the emphasis was again turned from being 'expert' to being 'red'.

Party control of the army

Particular attention has been paid to party control of the army. In 1959, China's Defence Minister was dismissed; probably because he thought it was necessary to get modern weapons, including nuclear weapons, from the Russians, even if that meant giving way to their opinions. His replacement was Lin Piao, one of the successful communist generals in the civil war. He has insisted that an army trained in guerrilla tactics, and armed with the thoughts of Mao Tse-tung, is better than any army that merely has weapons, however modern.

That did not prevent China exploding its first atomic device in late 1964, and firing a rocket with an atomic warhead two years later.

Spreading revolution

The Chinese since 1961 have been very active trying to stir up revolution in Africa, Asia and Latin America, by training so-called 'freedom fighters' and supplying them with money and weapons. They have done this not only in 'reactionary' countries or colonial territories, but, for instance, in Indonesia, a country which, until 1965, was very friendly to them. They have done their best to prevent any peaceful settlement of the war between Americans and Vietnamese communists in Vietnam.

21. *1966. Young Chinese celebrate the 'cultural revolution' with pictures of Mao Tse-tung and placards bearing the titles of books written by him*

The break with Russia

China's quarrel with Russia became open and abusive in 1963, and by 1965 the Chinese were denouncing the Russians as 'lackeys of American imperialism'. There have been occasional incidents on the long borders between the two countries. The Russians fear that one day the Chinese may try to reclaim the territory lost to Russia in several 'unequal treaties' in the nineteenth century. In appearance, the quarrel was still one between 'revolution' and 'coexistence' as the road forward for communism. But by 1966 it had become more and more like any ordinary quarrel between two powerful neighbour-states.

The 'cultural revolution'

In 1966 disagreements between China's leaders came into the open. Lin Piao emerged as the strong man of China, after Mao Tse-tung. Under his orders, mobs of young people and schoolchildren demonstrated, waving books of 'the thought of Mao Tse-tung'. The target of these 'red guards', as they were called, were certain leading communists, who were now denounced as 'reactionaries' and 'bourgeois rightists'; and anyone, or indeed anything (Buddhist statues, for instance), that could be given this description. Mao Tse-tung was glorified as 'the great teacher, great leader, great supreme commander and great helmsman', just as Stalin once was in Russia.

These activities were known as the 'cultural revolution'. They horrified not only the Russians, who were ferociously abused by the red guards, but even other Asian communist parties that had been friendly to the Chinese. After a few months of 'cultural revolution', the Russian and Chinese governments were hardly on speaking terms, and both were abusing each other in the same violent language that, before, they had reserved for the imperialists.

Yet once again it seemed that the Chinese communists, having taken two steps forward were going to take one step back. In early 1967, it was clear that they were trying to curb the enthusiasm of the red guards, who, in many parts of the country, had overthrown the party officials, and were quite out of control. Lin Piao's name was heard less often, and the

Prime Minister, Chou En-lai, who was generally believed outside China to be a man more interested in being 'expert' than in being 'red', came into prominence.

Yet the 'cultural revolution' had had one important effect. The red guards, who plastered the cities with political posters and ran their own newspapers, were in a way the heirs of the young students who shook up Chinese ideas in 1919–21 (see chapter 9). Though they all professed loyalty to the thought of Mao Tse-tung, for the first time since 1949, China had seen something like a democratic political debate – however ugly it looked – and had seen political actions taken by people on their own initiative, rather than on orders from above.

When this book was written, the 'cultural revolution' was still shaking China up. Even Chou En-lai was under attack, in what was evidently a fierce struggle for power between sections of the highest communist leadership. There was no certainty how the struggle would turn out. It might prove to be just a flash in the pan; it might be one of the most important events of modern Chinese history, and that, in mid 1967, seemed the more likely guess.

28. JAPAN UNDER AMERICAN OCCUPATION

MacArthur reforms Japan

For twenty years after its surrender in 1945, Japan played little part in Asian politics. But inside it many things changed.

It was occupied in 1945 by American troops under General Douglas MacArthur. The Japanese were allowed to govern themselves, but MacArthur insisted they must carry out American ideas. He wanted to make Japan a democratic country and to prevent it ever again becoming a danger to peace. So:

1. Japan lost its colonies, such as Korea, and also Manchuria and Formosa, which were given back to China.

2. The armed forces were abolished, and all military supplies and aircraft destroyed. A new constitution, introduced in 1947, declared that Japan would never have armed forces or go to war.

3. War criminals were tried. Seven Japanese leaders most to blame for starting the war were hanged. Thousands of less important people guilty of atrocities against prisoners of war and civilians in occupied countries were tried, and 700 executed.

4. Hundreds of thousands of people involved in pre-war politics and government were banned from public life.

5. The new constitution, written by Americans, guaranteed free speech, freedom for newspapers, secret voting in elections, votes for all adults (including women, who had not been allowed to vote) and many other democratic rights.

6. It also stated the basic principle of all democratic countries, that power belongs to the people as a whole and that the government acts in their name. Even the Emperor was said to 'derive his position from the will of the people' instead of being regarded as the supreme authority whom the people

should obey. Instead of being a remote figure, he began to visit factories and schools. Newspapers began to discuss him and his position.

7. The government was made fully responsible to the elected parliament, the Diet (which consists of a House of Representatives, elected every four years, or sooner, and a much weaker House of Councillors, half of whose members are elected every three years).

8. New laws reduced the power of the rich. Landowners were forced to sell most of their land at low prices, so that soon nearly all farmers owned their own farms. Trade unions were encouraged. The wealthy financiers who had controlled Japanese industry before the war – the *zaibatsu* – were forced to sell their shares to the government, which tried, with little success, to resell them to the public.

A partial success

These reforms looked good on paper. But some have not had much effect. They were imposed from outside, and democracy is not something that can be created by writing constitutions; it is a way of life that develops over many years, as it had in America. The Japanese had their own way of life. They were accustomed to respect people in authority. They were not much interested in the kind of party politics that the new constitution made possible. After the American occupation ended in 1952, there were signs of a return to a more Japanese way of doing things.

But the changes, like the Americans themselves, were generally popular. Most Japanese were glad to say goodbye to the irresponsible military rule of pre-war days that had brought them such disaster.

America's attitude changes

The American attitude to Japan changed rapidly. Instead of keeping Japan down and even dismantling its industry, they were soon trying to build it up; partly because they were having to spend a lot of money to keep Japan going, partly because they wanted it as an ally against communism. In 1949 they set out to revive Japanese industry. Laws against big business were changed, and by 1952 the *zaibatsu* were again at work. In

1950 and 1951 many of the people banned from politics were allowed to take part again.

Article 9 of the constitution, which forbade Japan to have armed forces, soon caused trouble to the Americans who had thought it up. Now they wanted Japan to take part in its own defence. Soon after the Korean War began, they encouraged the setting up of a 'national police reserve' of 75,000 men. This was the first step towards an army.

The peace treaty

In 1951, most of the countries that had been at war with Japan signed a peace treaty. The Russians refused to sign. Neither of the rival Chinese governments was invited; it was left to Japan to decide which one it would recognize. At the same time Japan and the United States signed a treaty allowing the Americans to station troops in Japan to defend it. This was in fact aimed against the Chinese communists.

When the peace treaty came into force in 1952, the occupation ended. Japan was again its own master.

29. THE NEW JAPAN

Industry grows

The most remarkable thing in Japan since 1952 has been the growth of industry. Japan has long since overtaken Britain. Its shipyards are the most efficient in the world. Its cameras and radios, which used to be poor imitations of Western ones, are now of the highest quality. Japanese motor-cycle manufacturers have driven some British ones out of business, and the Japanese since 1965 have launched a serious challenge to Western car and lorry manufacturers.

Asian or American?

With the growth of industry, Japan has become more like a Western country than an Asian one in some ways. Though the ordinary Japanese does not have the comforts most Westerners expect at home, he is far better off than nearly all other Asians. Tokyo, the capital, has the high office blocks, noise and traffic problems of other modern cities, and is now the largest city in the world. Many young Japanese have become partly Americanized. The very different kind of education that has been given since 1945 has made many young people grow up with quite different ideas from their parents.

Politics in Japan

Since 1945, the parliamentary form of government seems to have taken root in Japan. Except in 1947–48, the government has always been a 'conservative' one, while the main opposition has come from socialists. Both groups were divided among themselves. From 1945 to 1955 there were two main conservative parties, the Liberal Party and the Democratic Party. The leader of the Liberals was Shigeru Yoshida (born 1878), who was Prime Minister in 1946–47 and from 1948 to 1954. Long after he retired, he was still a powerful man in Japanese politics. The division between the two parties was really one of personalities, not of policies. In 1955 they united to form the Liberal-Democratic party, which has governed Japan ever since.

The socialists were supported mainly by the trade unions, which grew very rapidly in the first years of the American occupation. They too were divided, mainly over just how anti-American they should be. But in 1955, the two main socialist groups united, and formed the Japan Socialist Party.

Dangers to Parliament

There are some dangers to the parliamentary system:

1. Factions inside the parties. Especially among the Liberal-Democrats, Japanese politicians are more loyal to a particular leading politician than to the party as a whole. So if the leaders disagree, the party may be disrupted.

2. Demonstrations. The socialists have never managed to

22. *The world's first successful large-scale monorail system links Tokyo with its airport eight miles away. The world's fastest train also runs from Tokyo, covering 320 miles in three hours*

get more than about one-third of the votes in elections, so
since 1948 they have always been a minority in the Diet. They
have often chosen to organize great demonstrations against
laws they dislike, rather than argue against them in the Diet
and accept their defeat in the voting there. In 1960 the Socialist
Party split again because of this. A few of its members formed
a new Democratic-Socialist Party, arguing that these non-
parliamentary methods were wrong and would prevent the
socialists ever winning an election. They also thought the
socialists should be less closely tied to the trade unions. In
1965–66 there were signs that the main socialist party was
moving in the same direction.

3. The communists. They do not believe in parliamentary
methods. In 1946–49 communism was growing in Japan, but
the Americans then had leading communists banned from
politics and thousands of party members were dismissed from
government jobs and from broadcasting and newspaper
organizations. In 1950–52 the communists organized rioting
which antagonized many Japanese, and since then, though
their support has slowly increased, they have never won more
than a few seats in elections.

4. On the right wing, there are still some people with pre-
war militarist ideas. One of them in 1960 murdered the leader
of the socialists. There is also a Buddhist 'Clean Government'
party which has grown rapidly since 1964. Some people fear
that if there were a slump in Japan this might turn into a
dictatorial and anti-parliamentary party.

Japan in Asia

Even after the occupation ended, the Japanese did not take
much part in Asian politics. They stuck to business. But they
could not ignore their powerful neighbours, America, China
and Russia.

The United States and Japan

In 1953–54, anti-American feeling grew. Many Japanese disliked seeing so many American troops and bases around now
that the occupation was over. They disliked the Americans
urging that Japan itself must rearm. There was an outcry in
1954 when a Japanese fishing boat was covered in radio-active
dust from an American hydrogen bomb test.

In 1960 the socialists organized huge anti-American demonstrations to prevent a new treaty with the Americans being approved. Though it was more favourable to Japan than the treaty of 1951, the critics said it still gave the Americans far too much freedom to use bases in Japan for purely American purposes.

There is also resentment that the Americans continue to occupy the small Ryukyu islands, south of Japan's main islands, where they have a big airbase. The peace treaty of 1951 allowed this to continue. Now, say the Japanese, it is time it ended.

However the Japanese Liberal-Democrat governments have always kept on good terms with the Americans.

Japan and China

Japanese feelings towards communist China are very mixed. Japan does not recognize the communists as the legal government, yet it knows that it has to live next door to them.

After 1952, the Japanese government encouraged trade with China, but did so unofficially. In 1958, however, the Chinese suddenly cut off all trade, because the Japanese would not give it their official blessing. But after 1960 trade rapidly rose again. Though the Japanese government's official attitude sometimes causes difficulties, contacts between China and Japan are growing, and very few Japanese would oppose recognition of the communists, though that would make trouble with their rivals in Formosa.

China's best friends in Japan have been the Japanese communists. But even they were shocked by the 'cultural revolution' in China in 1966 (see chapter 27).

Japan and Russia

The Japanese have been on bad terms with Russia, mainly because the Russians in 1945 seized some small Japanese islands and have kept them. But this enmity is weakening. In 1966 the two countries agreed that Japanese money should be used to help develop Siberia, the far east of the Soviet Union, an area where the two countries have been rivals for so long. The Russians have decided that a nation as rich as Japan is one that cannot be ignored.

Japan and Korea

Most of the countries that the Japanese conquered have taken the same line; they do not greatly like Japan, but they want Japanese money to build up their industries. The one exception is South Korea, where the Japanese are much disliked. Though an agreement was eventually reached in 1965, after thirteen years of talks, for Japan to lend large sums to South Korea, many South Koreans, possibly most, saw this as a sell-out to their old colonial masters.

Growing strong again

Since 1964 Japan has started to take a more active place in the world. This powerful country is no longer willing to be simply the silent ally of the Americans. The Americans are not unhappy, though. Japan is a strong and non-communist country friendly to themselves. They would like to see it take its proper place in Asia, especially in 'defending' Asia against the Chinese.

Simply because it is so rich, Japan is bound to become more and more important. Its armed forces (called 'self-defence forces') though still small for its size have grown to 250,000 men. Its trade is enormous. The question is what this great country thinks its 'proper place' should be. It may not always be what the Americans expect.

30. PAST AND FUTURE

What the Europeans left behind

As empires go, the European empires in Asia did not last long: say 300 years in the Dutch East Indies, 200 years in India, 80 in limited areas of China, never at all in Japan. Though a few small colonies remained, one could take the Bandung meeting of 1955 as Asia's 'declaration of independence', the end of the European age.

Yet the Europeans had an enormous influence. Asian ways of thought and behaviour have been changed irreversibly. Oddly enough, most of the change occurred in the last sixty years, the years covered in this book, during which the European empires broke up.

And why

Yet that was not really so odd. The reason is that it was only during the last eighty or a hundred years that the European countries advanced so fast (particularly in industry and science) and that the gap between them and the Asians grew so great, that European power was bound to have a shattering effect on the Asian countries that it touched.

The effect was different in different places. In Japan, the Japanese simply set out to catch up with the Europeans (or Americans) by imitation. In India the British rulers created a new middle class, educated along British lines, to run the modern state that India was becoming. In China, the reaction was partly one of old-fashioned Chinese nationalism, partly, as in Japan, a determination to catch up.

But one thing was true in every case. The more the European influence, the more vigorously the Asians responded to it. They were shaken into trying to assert their own power. And the methods they used were the ones that they saw worked for the Europeans. At the moment of their greatest success, the Europeans were arousing the Asians to throw them out – and showing them how to do it.

The purpose of the first half of this book has been to describe, in detail, the results of this process and the different forms it took in different countries.

Winning power – and using it

The second part of the book has been about something different: about what happened when the imperialists (which for China meant the Japanese just as much as the Europeans) had gone home.

India and China, between 1910 and 1950, both won the right to govern themselves without outside interference or control. But having done that they were up against something which was quite as difficult: actually governing.

In India at least, the problems that the nationalists – the Congress Party – faced were far greater after independence than before. The same was even truer of the Muslim League in Pakistan. In China the processes of winning power and of actually using it went on side by side for forty years. Only in Japan (though it had other problems after its defeat in 1945) could the rulers concentrate simply on the use of the power they already had – which perhaps is why they misused it so badly.

What happens next?

No one can do more than guess what will happen to the great countries of Asia in the future; and guessing about them – except, perhaps, for Japan – is a good deal harder than guessing about Britain, say, or the United States. But one guess is fairly safe. These countries, China, Japan, India and Pakistan, already matter enormously to the rest of the world. In future they will matter still more.

INDEX

For Product Safety Concerns and Information please contact our EU
representative GPSR@taylorandfrancis.com
Taylor & Francis Verlag GmbH, Kaufingerstraße 24, 80331 München, Germany

www.ingramcontent.com/pod-product-compliance
Lightning Source LLC
Chambersburg PA
CBHW062041270326
41929CB00014B/2500

9 7 8 1 0 3 2 8 8 8 5 0 7